BOBBLES
&
PLUM

Contributors

PAUL R. SPIRING is both a Chartered Biologist and Physicist. He is employed by the Department for Children, Schools and Families (UK) to work as the Head of Biology at the European School of Karlsruhe in Germany. Paul is the joint author of two previous books entitled *On the Trail of Arthur Conan Doyle: An Illustrated Devon Tour* and *Bertram Fletcher Robinson: A Footnote to The Hound of the Baskervilles*. He has also compiled two further books entitled *Aside Arthur Conan Doyle*: *Twenty Original Tales by Bertram Fletcher Robinson* and *The World of Vanity Fair by Bertram Fletcher Robinson*. Paul is a member of numerous societies including The Devonshire Association, The Conan Doyle (Crowborough) Establishment, The Sherlock Holmes Society of London, La Société Sherlock Holmes de France, The Sydney Passengers and The Crew of the S.S. May Day.

ANDREW CROWTHER has been Secretary to the W.S. Gilbert Society since 2003. He maintains both the W.S. Gilbert Society website and *Babliophile*, a more personal celebration of Gilbert's life and work. Andrew is also the author of a study of Gilbert's works entitled *Contradiction Contradicted: The Plays of W.S. Gilbert*. He has written several plays including: *Smokeless Zone* (performed at Bradford University's Theatre in the Mill, 1999), *The Devil and the Deep Blue Sea* (Theatre in the Mill, 2000), *Welcome to Paradise* (Bradford Priestley Centre for the Arts, 2003) and *Funny Men* (Bradford Playhouse, 2008). Andrew is a P G Wodehouse enthusiast and believes *Right Ho, Jeeves* to be the funniest book ever written.

NORMAN MURPHY was a professional soldier who spent much of his time in Whitehall, which enabled him to spend six years of lunchtimes in the British Library identifying the origins of P G Wodehouse's characters and settings. His first book entitled *In Search of Blandings: The Facts Behind the Wodehouse Fiction* was released in 1981. Since then, he has written a logistic handbook for NATO, *The Reminiscences of the Hon. Galahad Threepwood* and *A Wodehouse Handbook: The World and Words of P.G. Wodehouse*. He is at present preparing a second edition of *One Man's London*.

TONY RING had a professional career in corporate taxation, the highlight of which was his election as President of the Chartered Institute of Taxation for 1990-1991. A Wodehouse enthusiast since the age of 11, he helped to found The P G Wodehouse Society (UK) in 1997 and edited its journal *Wooster Sauce* for ten years. Tony created a 600,000 word, eight-volume *Concordance* of Wodehouse's fiction, compiled *The Wit and Wisdom of P G Wodehouse*, and wrote *You Simply Hit Them with an Axe* about Wodehouse's tax problems, and *P G Wodehouse: In His Own Words* with Barry Day. In addition, for Galahad Books, he has published three books of unrepublished magazine stories by Wodehouse with explanatory introductions: the short story collection *Plum Stones* and the novels *The Luck Stone* and *A Prince for Hire*. He has contributed numerous articles to journals throughout the world concerning aspects of Wodehouse's work, is a member of Appreciation Societies in the USA, Netherlands, Belgium and Sweden, and has advised on the Wodehousean aspects of numerous other books, radio and television broadcasts and theatre productions.

Above. Bertram ('Bobbles') Fletcher Robinson (c. 1906).
Below. Pelham ('Plum') Grenville Wodehouse (1904).

BOBBLES
&
PLUM

Four Satirical Playlets by Bertram Fletcher Robinson & PG Wodehouse

Compiled by

Paul R. Spiring

ISBN-9781904312581

MX Publishing Ltd, 335 Princess Park Manor, Royal Drive,
London, N11 3GX
www.mxpublishing.co.uk

Book Jacket by Staunchdesign,
www.staunch.com

Dedication

The following eulogy to Bertram Fletcher Robinson was written by the English poet, writer and journalist, Jessie Pope. It was published in the *Daily Express* newspaper on Saturday 26 January 1907:

Good Bye, kind heart; our benisons preceding,
Shall shield your passing to the other side.
The praise of your friends shall do your pleading
In love and gratitude and tender pride.

To you gay humorist and polished writer,
We will not speak of tears or startled pain.
You made our London merrier and brighter,
God bless you, then, until we meet again!

Foreword

Lovers of literature, be they scholars or simply voracious readers, are always delighted when early, little known works are collected and republished. Scholars welcome a new opportunity for research, speculation and comparison between early and late works. Readers enjoy these too, but mainly they enjoy a good read, and they will find that here.

Whichever you are, we should join in congratulating Paul Spiring on producing this collection of four playlets written by two young men early in their careers. How astonished Bertram Fletcher Robinson and Pelham Grenville Wodehouse would be to find the playlets on which they collaborated more than a century ago, collected and republished in a new and very different century.

These were both young men, writers making their way in the world, finding their style, writing continuously at work and in their spare time. They were friends, having worked together at the *Daily Express* newspaper, had friends and acquaintances in common, and they continued the honourable tradition of swapping ideas and plots within their group. But they were still learning their trade – Wodehouse was just 22 when the first of these satires was published – and that makes them interesting to us now.

P G Wodehouse went on to develop his inimitable style and is today widely regarded as the greatest humorous writer of the 20th century, acknowledged by Evelyn Waugh as 'the Master of our profession'. With the advantage of longevity, Wodehouse wrote more than 70 novels, over 200 short stories and innumerable articles and pieces of journalism; his books are still in print and are loved throughout the world. Bertram Fletcher Robinson was not so fortunate. Just three weeks after the final playlet was published in '*The World*' on 1st January 1907, Bertram Fletcher Robinson died, aged just 36.

This collection of playlets, long lost to us, is a wonderful addition to the canon.

Hilary Bruce
Chairman, The P G Wodehouse Society (UK)
London, May 2009.

Preface

During the summer of 2005, I bought my first house at Ipplepen in Devon. A cursory investigation into the history of this beautiful village was to change my life for ever, and for the better. I discovered that Ipplepen was once home to Bertram Fletcher Robinson, a man whose name appears in an acknowledgement on the first page, of the first chapter, of the first edition, of perhaps the most popular detective story ever written, *The Hound of the Baskervilles*. But why, I asked myself, would the successful author, Arthur Conan Doyle seek assistance for his 'real creeper' from a seemingly unknown, 31 year-old journalist?

The answer to my question was lurking on library shelves throughout the United Kingdom. Fletcher Robinson held several degrees, was a serious contender for a place in the England rugby team, was a qualified Barrister and he had written 63 published items (1893-1901). Thereafter, he edited several famous periodicals and wrote a further 210 published items prior to his death in 1907, aged just 36 years. In short, he was a remarkable man and Conan Doyle had the acumen to see this long before most others.

During my research, I was struck by Fletcher Robinson's collaborations with other notable literary figures – often before their work was widely recognised: Rudolph Chambers Lehmann, Barry Pain, Owen Seaman, Max Pemberton, Wilfred Meynell, Jessie Pope and Pelham Grenville Wodehouse. In the case of Woodhouse, these collaborations became an annual affair. Hence, Fletcher Robinson and Wodehouse clearly enjoyed working together and felt that their association was mutually beneficial – this is also manifestly apparent within the following pages.

The purpose of this book is two-fold. Firstly, I wanted to reveal that the literary legacy of Fletcher Robinson extends beyond his involvement with Sir Arthur Conan Doyle. Secondly, I hope that it will serve to demonstrate that the genius, which Wodehouse later displayed was well-rooted by the tender age of 22 years.

Finally, I would like to thank the following individuals and organisations for their assistance with this book: Hilary Bruce (Chairman, The PG Wodehouse Society [UK]), Hugh Cooke (Head of English, The European School of Karlsruhe), Dr. John Deamer (Head of Philosophy, The European School of Karlsruhe), Graeme de Bracey Marrs (Robinson family), Alistair Duncan (Author), Shelah Duncan (British Library Research Service), Bob Gibson (staunchdesign), Stewart Gillies (British Library Research Service), Meade-King Robinson & Company Limited (Liverpool), Brian W. Pugh (Author & Curator of The Conan Doyle [Crowborough] Establishment), Arthur Robinson (Robinson family), Su Rumford, Marc Shepherd, Peter Straus (Rogers, Coleridge & White Literary Agency, London), Dr. Frances Willmoth (Archivist, Jesus College, The University of Cambridge), Claire Wilson (Rogers, Coleridge & White Literary Agency, London) and most especially Norman Murphy, Tony Ring and Andrew Crowther.

Paul R. Spiring
Karlsruhe, June 2009.

Contents

Introduction

The first ten years of the twentieth century were a good time to be a young writer. The Education Acts of the 1870s had produced a population that could read – and it wanted entertainment. Before the advent of radio, film or television, the principal home entertainments were the piano or the then-new gramophone. Everyone read voraciously, a habit that was met by 'penny dreadfuls', romantic magazines, 'sixpenny horrors', and weekly and monthly magazines, all full of short stories and advice on every topic under the sun. In 1901, there were over seven hundred weekly and monthly 'story' magazines published in the UK and London alone had nineteen daily morning papers and ten evening papers.

Bertram ('Bobbles') Fletcher Robinson (1870-1907) and Pelham ('Plum') Grenville Wodehouse (1881-1975) were, in many respects, typical of their time but, while Wodehouse's books still delight readers around the world, Fletcher Robinson's reputation as a writer faded after his early death.

Fletcher Robinson, the son of a merchant, was educated at Newton Abbot Proprietary College in Devon and went up to Jesus College, Cambridge, during 1890. He won three Rugby Blues and narrowly missed a Rowing Blue. Fletcher Robinson wrote for, and later edited, *Granta* at Cambridge and qualified as a barrister in 1896 but never practised. It is possible that he was encouraged to pursue a writing career by his uncle, John Richard Robinson, manager and editor of *The Daily News*, who was knighted in 1893. In 1895, Fletcher Robinson was commissioned to write the first volume of the *Isthmian Library of Sports and Pastimes*. The book, *Rugby Football*, was successful and in 1897, Fletcher Robinson became editor of the entire project and he edited a further eight volumes between 1897 and 1901.

During April 1900, Fletcher Robinson was sent to South Africa as a war correspondent for the new *Daily Express* newspaper; he travelled home during July 1900 with Dr. Arthur Conan Doyle. In April 1901, the pair met again on holiday in Cromer, Norfolk, where Fletcher Robinson told Conan Doyle a legend about a fearsome hound on Dartmoor. Conan Doyle was intrigued and he travelled to Devonshire to meet Fletcher Robinson and to research the area further. The coachman who accompanied them to Dartmoor was named Henry Baskerville, a name that Conan Doyle later used for a central character in his most famous detective story, *The Hound of the Baskervilles*.

There has been much controversy over the years as to how much of *The Hound of the Baskervilles* originated with Fletcher Robinson but, no matter how much or how little it was, the first edition thanks Fletcher Robinson thus:

> It was to your account of a West Country legend that this tale owes its inception. For this and for your help in all the details all thanks.
>
> Yours most truly
> A. Conan Doyle

Fletcher Robinson continued his journalist career as a freelance writer, making many contributions to the *Daily Express*, maybe because his friend Percy Everett was the literary editor. From September 1900, Fletcher Robinson seems to have had a regular *Daily Express* column till 1904, when he became editor of *Vanity Fair*. He retained this post till October 1906 when he was appointed editor of the weekly magazine *The World*. On 3 June 1902 he married Gladys Hill Morris, daughter of the well-known painter Philip Richard Morris; they had no children. He died on 21 January 1907, aged 36, at 44 Eaton Terrace, London of enteric fever followed by peritonitis.

The young P.G. Wodehouse had thoroughly enjoyed his schooldays at Dulwich College and had looked forward to going to Oxford. His father found he was unable to meet the fees, however, and had secured him a place in the Hong Kong and Shanghai Bank, where he began work in September 1900. He found himself among forty or so young men of similar background and he played for the Bank cricket and rugby teams, but writing was still his first priority. In the 1970s, Richard Perceval Graves (brother of the poet Robert Graves) recalled sharing lodgings back in 1901/2 with Wodehouse in Walpole Street, Chelsea, London. He remembered that every night after supper, Wodehouse vanished into the bathroom to avoid the postprandial chat and writing, writing, writing until midnight.

Between 1900 and 1908, Wodehouse kept a meticulous account of his literary earnings, the famous Cash Book, an invaluable source of information about his early years as a writer. During his time at the Bank, it was a matter of half a crown here and half a guinea there for two-line jokes, short humorous poems and the occasional short story. In *Over Seventy*, Wodehouse wrote: "There were so many morning papers and evening papers and weekly papers and monthly magazines that you were practically sure of landing your whimsical article on 'The Language of Flowers' or your parody of Omar Khayyam somewhere or other after about say thirty-five shots."

He found his humorous school stories did well in the new *Captain* boys' magazine, and his break came when W. Beach Thomas, who wrote the 'By the Way' humorous column of *The Globe* evening newspaper, started giving him an occasional day's work. On 9 September 1902, not yet twenty-one years old, Wodehouse made the big decision, to resign from the Bank and become a freelance writer. The trigger was almost certainly his imminent transfer to the Far East, which coincided with the offer of a three-week temporary employment with *The Globe* and the publication of his first book, a school story called *The Pothunters* published on 19 September. In the following eleven months, he had no less than thirty-nine pieces published in *Punch*, the ambition of every young writer, as well as numerous contributions in the *Daily Chronicle*. During that same period, Wodehouse also contributed to the *Royal*, *Windsor* and *Vanity Fair* magazines.

In August 1903, Wodehouse secured a regular position as a writer for the 'By the Way' column of *The Globe* newspaper. *The Globe* paid three guineas a week and Wodehouse finished his column by noon, which left the rest of the day for his freelance work, a situation that he fully exploited.

We will probably never know when Wodehouse and Fletcher Robinson first met, but a likely period is September/October 1903, when Wodehouse wrote the first of his 'Parrot' poems for the *Daily Express*, the same newspaper that employed Fletcher Robinson. Wodehouse rarely wrote of political matters and then only in satirical terms but the period between 1900 and 1911 were years of turmoil when new issues divided Parliament and public opinion as they had not done for decades. Particularly notable events included the election of the first Labour MPs, a split within the Liberal Unionist Party, resignations from the Cabinet (a Conservative-led Unionist alliance with the Liberal Unionist Party) and the growing strength of both the Liberal Party and Irish Parliamentary Party.

Outside Parliament, there was increasing displacement of horse-drawn transport by lorries and motor cars; and, encouraged by King Edward VII, a radical change in the customs of Society. The four Bobbles & Plum playlets are a satirical contemporary view of these events.

They are nearly forgotten today, but the Parrot poems became a national craze and it would be no exaggeration to say they influenced the political history of the country. On 9 September 1903, Joseph Chamberlain shocked the nation by resigning from the Cabinet and announcing his intention of opposing it on the issue of Imperial Preference versus Free Trade. Alarmed at the growing power of a Germany unified by Bismarck, he sought to turn the British Empire into a powerful trading bloc by imposing import tariffs on other countries. When he realised the Conservative-led administration would never agree, he decided to go it alone though it meant splitting the Liberal Unionist Party. Free Trade had been the norm for sixty years and Chamberlain was opposed by many Conservatives and most Liberals who voiced their view that the tariffs would raise food prices with the slogan: "Your food will cost you more".

On 30 September 1903, the front page of the *Daily Express* featured a poem that imitated Edgar Allen Poe's 'The Raven' in which four verses end: "Quoth the raven, 'Nevermore'". The *Daily Express* poem featured a parrot giving his opinion on the Tariff-Reform idea and ending each verse with the words: "Your food will cost you more." The parrot continued to make his views known on the front page daily until 16 November and intermittently till mid-December, always with each verse ending with the phrase that soon became a nation-wide slogan. The poems were published anonymously but according to the Wodehouse Cash Book, he wrote nine Parrot poems in

October 1903 at a guinea each, eight in November and two in December (some of them were re-printed in *The Parrot and Other Poems* (London: Hutchinson, 1988). Historians now agree that the strong feelings aroused by the issue and the dissension among the Conservatives were a major factor in the Liberal landslide election victory of 1906.

Fletcher Robinson may also have contributed to the Parrot poems in the *Daily Express*; he certainly wrote light verse though many would say Wodehouse had the edge over him in this regard. One feature that did differentiate their writing was their choice of subjects. Wodehouse occasionally wrote serious articles on schools, Rugby football and boxing but seems to have realised early on that his forte was humour and light novels.

Fletcher Robinson covered a wider range. Although he had been a salaried employee, like Wodehouse he also engaged in freelance work and between 1893 and his death, he wrote poems, songs, playlets, numerous articles on many topics, fifty-five short stories and three books as well as collaborating on four others. In 1902, for example, he wrote six humorous articles for *Pearson's Magazine* that satirised the new sporting fashions of the time. In 1904, the same journal published a scholarly article by him on Bronze Age remains on Dartmoor (to which he had conducted Conan Doyle) and during the following year, it featured a mystery story by him about a prisoner escaping from Dartmoor prison. In 1904, he also published a series of stories featuring a detective named Addington Peace and these tales were later serialised in several American newspapers.

If Fletcher Robinson had not known of Wodehouse's work before he wrote the Parrot poems in December 1903, he certainly seems to have recognised its merits afterwards.

Wodehouse had had six contributions in *Vanity Fair* in 1903 but, when Fletcher Robinson became editor, probably in May 1904, Wodehouse became a regular contributor.

During 1905, it appears that Wodehouse and Fletcher Robinson had a temporary falling-out. Wodehouse's record of earnings, the famous Cash Book, is meticulous in its entries. He put down payments received for everything that he wrote and when he lost one day's pay from *The Globe*, it was noted. The Cash Book shows that he submitted three contributions to *Vanity Fair* during April 1905, another in May and another in June. They all appeared in the magazine but a couple do not appear to have been paid for. We will probably never know what happened. Perhaps *Vanity Fair* was in financial trouble and couldn't pay and, if Fletcher Robinson had become a friend, Wodehouse may have been unwilling to embarrass him? Not until October is there a Cash Book note of two pieces for *Vanity Fair*, both of half a guinea each. Wodehouse also received the unusually large sum of eight guineas for his part in the collaboration with Fletcher Robinson over *A Winter's Tale: King Arthur and his Court* (*Vanity Fair*, 14 December 1905).

Between May 1902 and late 1905/early 1906, Wodehouse kept a notebook, 'Phrases and Notes', in which he jotted down ideas, remarks and comments on interesting people that he met. In one entry Wodehouse wrote: 'I suggest to Miss Pope that she and I should call on Fletcher Robinson together and bully him for more payment. She says "Will it do any good?" I say "It won't do <u>him</u> any good." It seems likely that Wodehouse wrote these remarks during mid-February 1906. During the previous month, he had made two contributions to *Vanity Fair* but the Cash Book records that he got only six shillings and eight shillings for them. This was a big drop from the half guinea he was used to receiving. Perhaps he and Miss Pope* did beard Fletcher Robinson in his editorial den and, if they did so, it seems to have worked for Wodehouse whose next contribution was rewarded with the standard half guinea.

Despite these financial quibbles, Wodehouse and Fletcher Robinson appear to have remained good friends. During October 1906, Fletcher Robinson resigned from *Vanity Fair* and he was appointed the editor of a London-based weekly called *The World*. That same month, Wodehouse made his final contribution to *Vanity Fair* and his first contribution to *The World*. He continued to write for *The World* until February 1907, just several weeks after the death of Fletcher Robinson.

In contrast to Fletcher Robinson, whose career was so wretchedly curtailed, Wodehouse wrote professionally for over seventy years, achieving major success as a novelist, writer of short stories and lyricist in musical comedy and, for a time between the wars, achieving a fair degree of success as an adapter of other people's work for the straight theatre. But just as Fletcher Robinson died at 36, so Wodehouse's writing to a similar age can be regarded as a long apprenticeship as he tested out different styles and techniques, wrote on different subjects, and took advice from different people as to how he should approach a professional writing career.

* Jessie Pope (1868-1941) was well-known in the period before the First World War as the writer of short humorous poems on domestic matters. In some respects, her light verses were the feminine equivalent of Wodehouse's and written in a similar vein. Pope was quoted once as being the 'foremost woman humorist' and she has some forty books listed in the British Library Catalogue. Pope clearly held Fletcher Robinson in high regard because she wrote him an affectionate eulogy that was published in the *Daily Express* on 26 January 1907 (see p. VII).

By 1909, Wodehouse had begun to follow three distinct strands of penmanship. As a journalist, he wrote extensively in prose and verse for the numerous daily, weekly and monthly papers and journals which were eager for contributions; as a fiction-writer, he concentrated initially on short stories and novels about school life before moving on to other settings with which he was familiar – a bank, and a newspaper office – and, after visiting the United States of America, he even wrote two novels containing significant criticism of the corruption that was then endemic in the New York City government and police force.

Advice from J. M. Barrie to write about what the market wanted, which he pursued particularly whilst in the USA, sent him off track for a while, but once he had made a break-through into the world of American musical comedy in 1916, he threw off that yoke and found his niche as the comic author who has by now already entertained four or five generations. Musical comedy was, indeed, the third strand of his budding career – he was invited by Owen Hall to write a lyric for the successful show *Sergeant Brue*, and a couple of years later was given a permanent evening job as topical lyric-writer at the Aldwych (and then Hicks and Gaiety) theatres.

As has already been mentioned, in the early days of the century, Woodhouse took the view that he should write in the evenings while working full-time at the Hong Kong and Shanghai Bank during the day, with a view to earning sufficient to justify the risk of becoming a full-time writer. By the end of 1907 he had written for more than 40 publications, his work ranging from short verses to serialised novels, and he had earned more than £500 from his writing for three years in a row.

The subject-matter within Wodehouse's work varied enormously, and it included a few reasonably serious, descriptive pieces usually on some aspect of sport. For the magazine *VC* he conducted a series of interviews, most importantly with Fletcher Robinson's friend, Sir Arthur Conan Doyle, in July 1903. But he rarely wrote on overtly political subjects – his occasional forays towards the public arena being satirical references to a specific politician's reported activity or speech. Wodehouse's preferred topics were the theatre, sport and trivial day-to-day news reports on which he could practise his rhyming skills by creating a humorous commentary in verse.

It is something of a surprise, therefore, to see Wodehouse credited with writing so many of the Parrot poems in the *Daily Express*. They are written with skill and use different rhyming and scansion techniques, and obviously required an element of constructive thought, but it would not be fair to suggest that the verses were representative of his committed political views! These are perhaps more fairly expressed in a six-line verse from *Songs on the Situation* in *Books for Today and Books for Tomorrow* (February 1904):

> Upon the fiscal question I
> Hold no decided views.
> I sometimes read the *Daily Mail*,
> Sometimes the *Daily News*,
> And thoroughly agree with each
> That nought is true but what they teach.

The first of the four Bobbles & Plum playlets is entitled *A Fiscal Pantomime: The Sleeping Beauty*. Interestingly, it contains the lyric 'We are a happy Free Food League. We are! We are! We are!'. Later, Wodehouse wrote a poem entitled, *The Phalanx* which is a wry comment upon the differences that existed between members of the 1905 Cabinet. Each verse of this poem closes with the line 'We are a happy Cabinet. We are! We are! We are!'.

It became clear from incidental comments in Wodehouse's writing throughout his career that he was very suspicious of modern art, modern poetry and the trends in theatrical writing portrayed by such playwrights as Ibsen. For example, in *Summer Lightning* (1929), Wodehouse wrote 'She looked like something that might have occurred to Ibsen in one of his less frivolous moments.' Wodehouse believed that the theatre should provide entertainment for audiences whose representative member might be the 'tired business man', and undoubtedly that was a popular view at the time. Hence, his willingness to undertake the second Bobbles & Plum playlet, *Our Christmas Pantomime: Little Red Riding Hood*, with its alleged contributions by Messrs Pinero, Maeterlinck, Jones and Ibsen is not a surprise – Wodehouse would have felt more comfortable writing this piece. We can glimpse his real thoughts within the following limerick from *The Books of Today and The Books of Tomorrow* (October 1907):

There was a great author named Jones
Who spoke of our drama with groans.
But his own play, they state,
Isn't anything great
(Note: In glass houses, never throw stones.)

The third Bobbles & Plum playlet, *A Winter's Tale: King Arthur & His Court*, was a purely political satire, and Wodehouse only contributed lyrics to it – at least that is what he recorded in his Cash Book that he was paid for.

Wodehouse's continued indifference to the political scene is reflected in another contribution to *The Books of Today and The Books of Tomorrow* (February 1906), in which he writes about the fun of the election hustings, and the relief that the election campaign is over, before wryly observing that unless there is shifty political trickery, the rolling years will bring pleasures anew, with 'The stir and the fight and the polling, Opponents a fellow can boo.'

The fourth and final Bobbles & Plum playlet, *The Progressive's Progress: Some Memories of 1906*, satirised the dramatically increasing expenditure of the fairly new London County Council (then controlled by the centre-left Progressive Party) coupled with a visit by a delegation from the Paris Municipal Council to London in late 1905. Two incidental targets were the Suffragette movement and the shock with which Society (as opposed to the general public) reacted to the phenomenon of musical comedy actresses marrying into the aristocracy. The latter is specifically referred to in *Lady Highflyer* song in Scene II.

The theme of the aristocracy having romantic involvement and even marriage ties with musical comedy stars and chorus girls was something with which Wodehouse would become very familiar both in the UK and in an equivalent sense in the USA. He worked with Gertie Millar, who became the Countess of Dudley (and indeed, lived next door to her in Le Touquet in the 1930s), and later in the USA with Marion Davies, who achieved the American equivalent by her liaison with William Randolph Hearst. It was not really a political matter, and he would have felt very much at home commenting on the phenomenon in this play.

There are two matters worthy of further consideration with respect to all four Bobbles & Plum playlets. The first is to postulate whether indeed Wodehouse was essentially responsible for the verse and Fletcher Robinson for the dialogue. Wodehouse was already an experienced verse-writer, for at times he produced almost weekly verses for *Punch*, the *Daily Chronicle, Books of Today and Books of Tomorrow*, as well as *Vanity Fair* and the *Daily Express* Parrot series. He had learned the art at Dulwich College, and was to return to it intermittently for the rest of his life. The second point is to note how much of the verse seems to the inexpert, at least, to carry the rhythms of Gilbert and Sullivan lyrics. Wodehouse is on record as having seen G&S operettas whenever he could, and having admired the lyric-writing of Gilbert, so this might be supporting evidence for the first proposition. But as with so many speculations of this sort – it doesn't really matter!

Fletcher Robinson was just over eleven years older than Wodehouse, and his record shows that his was a well-liked writing style. If we assimilate the progress of his career to that of Wodehouse, we can say that his death came just as he would have completed an apprenticeship, and that he would have been preparing to embark on the most productive and compelling part of his output. From what we can read in the four Bobbles & Plum playlets, it is clear that both writers could apply themselves to satirical comment on current affairs with skill and considerable humour. But contemporary satire does not last, and it is to be regretted that, unlike Wodehouse, Fletcher Robinson was not able to leave a substantial corpus of wide-ranging work by which he could be fairly judged.

It is tempting to speculate what would have happened if Fletcher Robinson had not died so suddenly. He might have continued in editorial roles and commissioned further work from Wodehouse; he might, encouraged by the modest success of his Addington Peace stories, have turned increasingly to detective fiction and encouraged Wodehouse to do the same. We shall never know. But at least we can enjoy the four playlets they wrote together which, even after a century, have a wit and charm we can still appreciate today.

Norman Murphy
with Tony Ring
April 2009.

A FISCAL PANTOMIME

THE SLEEPING BEAUTY

DAILY EXPRESS, LONDON
25TH DECEMBER 1903

A FISCAL PANTOMIME.

THE SLEEPING BEAUTY.

The Performance which will Bring Joy to the Hearts of the Free Food League.

The Free Fooders have good reason to complain of the pantomimes. The ballad of the Cobden Club has yet to be written, and instead of ditties in praise of the alien the "principal boys" in the various houses of entertainment are preparing songs suggesting that we should do by the Yank and German as they now do to us; that foreign dumping is not a thing to be encouraged when it throws the British workman out of a job at Christmas; and that Chamberlain is the man who will set our trade in order.

We are able to-day to make an exclusive announcement that should be received with enthusiasm by the Cobden Press. The Free Food League have obtained leave to use the stage at Ch-tsw-rth (by the kind permission of the Duke of D-v-nsh-r-) for their very own pantomime, which has been written to display the amazing conversion of the Duke to Free Food League principles by the agency of Sir Michael Hicks Beach and Sir Henry Campbell-Bannerman. The foiling of the Tariff Reform League is also politely indicated.

THE SLEEPING BEAUTY.

A Pantomime in Two Acts.

CHARACTERS.

THE SLEEPING BEAUTY..The Duke of D-v-nah-r.
HER NURSE.....................The "Standard."
MICHAEL (principal boy)......Sir M H-cks B—ch.
HENRY (second boy)...............Sir H. C-B.
A PLOUGHMAN (first walking gentleman)
                                Lord Ros-b-ry.
A GHOST.........................The Parrot.
A DRAGON..............The Tariff Reform League.
MEMBER OF COBDEN CLUB....Herr Spoofheimer
CHORUS............The Rest of the Cobden Club.

Scene I.—Outside the pavilion of the
Sleeping Beauty.
Scene II.—Inside the above pavilion.
Time.—October 1, the day before the
Duke resigned and on which pheasant
shooting began.

ACT I.

To the right is the pavilion of the Sleeping Beauty, beside which the Tariff Reform
League Dragon dozes with one eye open,
Michael and Henry are discovered (badly)
left.

MICHAEL: Frankly, my dear Henry, that
dragon alarms me.

HENRY: True, sir knight, had you been
but Lord George, then indeed——

MICHAEL, Why bring in the Lord George?
A man with so marked an air of resignation
as he wears would never tackle it.

HENRY: Pardon me, but it was to Lord
George Sanger I referred as being a re-
nowned wild beast tamer.

MICHAEL: Someone at the Hippodrome, I
suppose. The question is, Can we get into
the place or not? If I can but pass that
brute at the door I have a master word that
will awake the Beauty from her slumbers.
But, mark you, who comes here?

(Enter the Ploughman carrying imple-
ments of agriculture about him. He halts
and gazes at the pavilion with a languish-
ing glance.)

2

HENRY: I know the man. Trust him not.
MICHAEL: See, he directs a friendly look
towards us. I want all the friends I can
get, Henry—that's why I love you so
passionately. I will inquire of him as to
his purpose. Fair bucolic (addressing the
Ploughman), are you with us or against
us ? Does Chamberlain charm you, or art
thou a Free Fooder in embryo?
THE PLOUGHMAN (vaguely): What do you
think of it all?
MICHAEL: That's what I'm asking you.
Come, confess, explain, define yourself.
THE PLOUGHMAN: I will sing it to you.

THE PLOUGHMAN'S SONG.

A wandering ploughman I
 Of habits literary.
Through furrow solitary
My lonely plough I ply,
 Exposing Joseph's sins
In quaint and courtly diction;
I hold not Fact, but Fiction.
 The quality that wins.
Are you in contemplative mood?
 I'll jest with you.

 Oh, willow, willow.
O'er fiscal problems do you brood?
 I'll do so, too.
 Oh, willow, willow.
Within the House of Peers
I charm attentive ears,
 My celebrated sneer's surpassed by few.
 Oh, willow, willow.
But if strenuous activity is needed,
If my party calls their Rosebery to the
 fray,
I let their cries of "Lead us!" pass un-
 heeded,
Or check them with a mild "some other
 day!"
The papers drop a hint that I am shirking;
 I really don't care greatly if they do;
But at talking (as opposed to honest work-
 ing)
 I yield, as I remarked before, to few.

So if you call for an empty jest,
 I'll make one while you wait:
I'll quip and quirk and pun and the rest
For as long as you please with infinite zest;
 But work is a thing I hate.
 Yeo-ho, heave-ho!
 Work is a thing I hate.

(The Tariff Reform League Dragon yawns,
displaying excellent teeth.)

MICHAEL (to the Ploughman): In the name
of Cobden, get out of this! Don't you see
the dragon?

(The Ploughman retires at the double,
glancing nervously over his shoulder.)

MICHAEL: He's no good to anybody, that
chap. Yet he's not without ability, and he
looks a likely fellow with his hands. I
can't understand him.

HENRY (quoting): "There are more things
in heaven and earth, Horatio, than are
dreamt of in your philosophy."

(The stage instantly becomes pitch dark;
the pair huddle together in great alarm.)

MICHAEL (irritably): That comes from
quoting Hamlet. What a silly ass you are,
Henry!

(Enter the Ghost of the Parrot.)

MICHAEL (trembling): Oh, my prophetic
soul! The Parrot!

HENRY: What would'st thou, bird?

THE GHOST: I will sing to you.

THE PARROT'S SONG.

When I was alive you cried oncore
To my squawk, "Your food will cost you
        more,"
And bread that you falsely named as free
Seemed just the very best bread to me.
An influential bird was I
'Mid Cobdenite inanity;
And every day was I wont to sing
Of woes that Tariff Reform would bring.
Repentance now on my head I pour,
For I know that food will NOT cost more.

4

And every day I raised that cry,
Though I couldn't exactly tell you why,
For when they asked me how I knew
I only replied that it was true,
And I really didn't know what to say
When Joe declared on a fateful day
That the reason our commerce had decayed
Was because we stuck to our Unfree Trade;
So I ended my life; but I now confess
That I know your food will cost you LESS!

MICHAEL: Out, serpent that I warmed in my jaegers!

HENRY. Aroint the wretch!

(Parrot disappears amid subdued laughter from the Dragon. The lights are switched on again.)

HENRY: Well, what are you going to do? You can't stay here all day, you know.

MICHAEL: Yet I like not the Dragon the more from the contemplation of it. Isn't there a way round?

HENRY: Not that I know of. But, hist, I have an idea. Yonder is a patriotic dragon that loves his country. Let us charm him with a patriotic song.

MICHAEL: Well, you sing it.

HENRY: I cannot remember one at the moment. Our party was never very strong on such things. But here comes a member of the Cobden Club who may oblige us.

(Enter Herr Spoofheimer followed by other foreign members of the Cobden Club, talking together in Volapuk—the only language in which they can communicate.)

MICHAEL: Well met, mein Herr. Canst thou tip us a stirring stave, some patriotic ballad that may conciliate this dragon here?

HENRY: Try "John Bull's Store."

HERR SPOOFHEIMER: Mein friends, I know him not—dot store. Und yet will I dry somewhat dot may suit your purpose.

5

SONG OF THE COBDEN CLUB.

Let Britannia rule der see
  And der land and air
(Hans and Hermann, you and me
Know goot cusdomers may be
  Best discovered dero).

Chorus by the Club—

Vive der land of liberty!
Hoch! Der beople ever free,
Free to spend der coin they've made
And uncommon Free in trade!

Cheer, my boys, for Englant's sake,
  Boast her glorious name
(If she buys der things we make
We will mooch goot money take),
  Honour Britain's fame.

Chorus as before.

Any nation could she thump
  If it came to fight
(If she says we must not dump.
Gott, it gives me quite der hump
  Joost to think she might!)

Chorus as before.

Britons never fear a foe
  To our Empire's realm
(Brothers, you and I would go
To der workhouse should this "Joe"
  Ever take the helm).

Chorus (with enthusiasm).

Cheer for Englant, one and all,
So her loyal Teutons bawl
Englant long will rule der main
If she keeps out Chamberlain!

(Dragon rushes at them with a snarl, and
they fly in different directions amid cries
of, " Ach so! " " Mille tonnerre! " " Guess
not! " As Henry runs in front of the
pavilion a note is thrown from within. He
reads it with joy.)

HENRY (to Michael): There is a way
round, my dear Michael. A sure friend
from within sends us word. Let's away.

CURTAIN.

Act II.

(Within the pavilion. The Sleeping Beauty (The Duke of D-v-nsh-r-) lies upon a conch in the centre of the stage, snoring pleasantly. Beside him sits the "Standard" Nurse, fanning him with a copy of that paper. Through the curtains (right) the tip of the T.R.L. Dragon's tail is visible. The Nurse commences a slumber song to a tuneful melody.

SLUMBER SONG.

Aristocratic creature,
Noble in more than feature,
Do not awake
Lest you make a mistake
Which might be quite a bore!
Now by your sneer inaction
You have confused each faction,
All are in doubt
What you're thinking about
While you snore, dear, snore!

Trade! It is low, disgracing;
Do not, your blood debasing.
Stoop to inquire
If our imports are higher
Than they were e'er before.
Leave to the trader shoddy
Facts which that vulgar body
Loves to pore over.
For you are in clover
While you snore, dear, snore!

Let well alone, my dearest,
That which exists is clearest,
Be not a changer,
For dark is the danger
In what was not done of yore.
Naught but acutest worry
Rises from haste and hurry.
Sleep on in quiet;
We'll ward off all riot
While you snore, dear, snore!

(As the "Standard" Nurse concludes Michael and Henry crawl in through a slit at the back of the tent.)

MICHAEL: This is deuced undignified, Henry. In short, it likes me not.

HENRY: Yet, my dear comrade, it was the only way.

7

MICHAEL:

Well, we're here now, and there she lies,
The cynosure of Michael's eyes.
If I can wake her, then, indeed,
She will be useful at our utmost need.
Allied great Beach and Cavendish, I ween,
Will place poor Joseph in the soup tureen.
How little thinks he——

HENRY: Look out. Isn't that the tail of
the Tariff Reform League Dragon at the
door of the tent?

MICHAEL: So it is. Let us walk circum-
spectly lest we tread upon it. But, hist, we
are observed!

THE "STANDARD" NURSE: Welcome, my
bonny Michael. But who is this beside you?
I like not his looks.

MICHAEL: Misery makes man acquainted
with strange bed-fellows. 'Tis my old
enemy, Henry, yclept C.-B.; yet now my
friend. . (Aside.) For this night only if it
please you, nurse.

HENRY: That's not the proper way to talk
about me. I will tell you who I am, and
that right swiftly.

HENRY'S SONG.

You may talk about your Wellingtons and
    Nelsons;
  You may rave about your Cannings and
    your Pitts;
    But ne'er did Nature plan a man
    So great as Campbell-Bannerman.
He beats the men I've mentioned into fits.
If you wish to take up arms against Pro-
    tection,
  Go! follow where his standard is un-
    furled.
    Though his methods may be tentative,
    He's grandly representative
Of quite the greatest party in the world.
    Vote for C.-B.! Oh, vote for C.-B.!!
    For the loaf that is large and the
    trade that is free.
      He is going to crush Joe
      (Tho' just when I don't know),
  So do vote for our peerless C.-B.

He may not be a genius at statistics;
  But everyone knows figures are a bore;
   A man supremely pat I call
   In matters mathematical
  Who, adding two to two, can make it four.
He may not be so accurate as Joseph;
  He may serve up facts quite queerly now
   and then;
  But perfect truth's a rarity,
  So exercise your charity;
A genius is not like other men.

    So vote for C.-B.! Oh, vote for C.-B.!!
    For the loaf that is large and the
    trade that is free.
      Hurry home and peruse
      What they say in the " News,"
And you're certain to vote for C.-B.

"STANDARD" NURSE (aside): A Radical,
as I live! My mind misgives me! (Address-
ng them.) May I ask which of you is the
_uitor to my dear lady here?

MICHAEL: I am, of course. Henry, get out
of the limelight. You play second fiddle,
you know, and don't you forget it!

HENRY (deeply offended): Enough! I'm off.

(Henry crawls back through the slit in
the tent with great dignity.)

MICHAEL (regretfully): Yet he was not
without his uses. But now, dear nurse, to
business. Allow me to approach yonder
beauty. I hold the master word that may
awake her.

"STANDARD" NURSE: May fortune, kind
attend you!

(Michael approaches the Sleeping Beauty
to slow music. Pausing by her ear he col-
lects himself for an effort.)

MICHAEL (crescendo): CHAMBERLAIN IS THE
MAN!

SLEEPING BEAUTY (drowsily): Hello—
what's that?

MICHAEL: Chamberlain is THE leader of
the Unionist party!

SLEEPING BEAUTY (waking up): Not on
your life, fair sir.

9

MICHAEL: He is IT! The country acclaims him as its leader.

SLEEPING BEAUTY (on her feet by now): You don't say so! And no one told me?

MICHAEL: He stole a march——

SLEEPING BEAUTY: The thief!

MICHAEL: He is! He stole a march upon you while you indulged in a well-merited repose. To arms, my ducal one!

SLEEPING BEAUTY (confused): Whose arms?

MICHAEL: Why, mine. (They embrace.)

SLEEPING BEAUTY: I will resign. I do not care what they say. I'll write letters to the papers. I don't care for Joe. Who's afraid? I will be as bold as radium and twice as active.

MICHAEL (aside): I hope he'll stick to it.

"STANDARD" NURSE: Bless you, my children!

TRIO:

SLEEPING BEAUTY, MICHAEL, and "STANDARD" NURSE.

MICHAEL:

Our troubles now are at an end; uncertainty
  is past.
How wonderful it is to think that she's
  awake at last!
We'll live together evermore without a
  hitch or jar—

ALL:

We are a happy Free Food League! We are!
  We are! We are!

"STANDARD" NURSE:

I never dreamed I should have been selected
  for this task.
My cup of joy is brimming o'er; I've nothing
  more to ask.
I do not think I ever felt so wholly up to
  par—

ALL:

We are a happy Free Food League! We are!
  We are! We are!

SLEEPING BEAUTY:
I feel a little sleepy still. I cannot quite
make out
Exactly what has happened, and just what
it's all about—

MICHAEL:
But still, in such a league as this, that's
not the slightest bar—

ALL:
We are a happy Free Food League! We are!
We are! We are!

MICHAEL:
We'll stump the country end to end; from
south to north we'll go;
We will not leave a single soul to vote for
poor old—

SLEEPING BEAUTY:
Joe!

"STANDARD" NURSE:
My leaders, too, I think, will make him
curse his evil star—

ALL:
We are a happy Free Food League! We are!
We are! We are!

(As they dance round a roar is heard
without.)

SLEEPING BEAUTY: I say, Michael, that's
a nasty noise. What is it?

MICHAEL: It is—er—a sort of—er—dragon.
In short, the Tariff Reform League Dragon.
It's a vicious brute.

SLEEPING BEAUTY: Oh, dear! oh, dear!
It's so fond of Joe, too! What are we
to do?

"STANDARD" NURSE: If I might suggest
—there is the hole at the back of the tent.

MICHAEL: The very thing!

(They crawl out through the back way as
the curtain falls.)

B. FLETCHER ROBINSON.
P. G. WODEHOUSE.

OUR CHRISTMAS PANTOMIME

LITTLE RED RIDING HOOD

'*VANITY FAIR*'

8TH DECEMBER 1904

Our Christmas Pantomime.

LITTLE RED RIDING HOOD; OR, THE VIRTUOUS BRITISH PUBLIC AND THE SMART SET WOLF.

By B. FLETCHER ROBINSON AND P. G. WODEHOUSE.

CHARACTERS.

LITTLE RED RIDING HOOD: The Virtuous British Public.
GRANDMOTHER: Mrs. Grundy.
GOOD FAIRY: Mr. W. T. Stead.
DEMONS: Messrs. Pinero, Maeterlinck, Jones, Ibsen.
HUNTERS: Messrs. Benson, R. J. Campbell, Sutro, Mesdames Corelli and Rita.
And the
WOLF: The Smart Set.

ACT I.

(*An ordinary wood, consisting of trees kindly lent by His Majesty's Theatre. Vista to left showing* MRS. GRUNDY'S *cottage in the distance.*)

(*Enter the authors, disguised as a Prologue.*)

The PROLOGUE, *with the modesty of conscious merit noticeable in its demeanour:*

To us, my friends, your kind attention lend,
Fable our means, morality our end.
Does this Smart Set, of whom we daily read,
Live but to gamble, motor, flirt, and feed?
Would it destroy the virtue which we find
So patent in the British Public's mind?
Is it but Wolf indeed, who from its den
Has rushed to swallow all the Upper Ten,
While even commoners in danger be?
Is this a fact? Or does sheer jealousy
Inspire the critics who upon it fall,
Since wealth in others is abhorred by all?
We do not know, nor do we think that you
Have better information—so adieu.

(*Exit the* PROLOGUE *hastily. Enter the Virtuous British Public as* LITTLE RED RIDING HOOD.)

12

LITTLE RED RIDING HOOD :

I am so tired and my feet are sore,
So far from home I've never been before—
At least without a proper chaperone,

(*Looking about.*)

And now I feel so very much alone.
'Tis but the sense of duty which to-day
Impels me on my slightly nervous way;
For in this wood a horrid Wolf resides,
Called the Smart Set, and woe, indeed, betides
She who should meet him, so at least I'm told,
By ladies young and leader-writers old.
Still, e'en a wolf should ever have his due,
And so of him I now will sing to you.

SONG : LITTLE RED RIDING HOOD.

I've heard of the ways of that wonderful coterie
    Known as the Smart Set to all in the land;
They race through a life that is Bridge-y and motor-y—
    Things that I've read of, but don't understand.
Their code of morality's dreadful and sinister,
    Quite a disgrace to our civilised times :
Morphia and so on they freely administer;
    Breakfast in bed is the least of their crimes.
All their existence unpleasantly garish is,
Shocking the vicars of neighbouring parishes;
Men of position and ladies of quality
Spend day and night in a round of frivolity.
    Rarely, they say, has the sun ever shone
    O'er such terrible, scandalous, sad goings-on.

        The scandals and sins of our modern society
            Beat Greece and Rome in extent and variety;
        Egypt and Babylon look very small,
            The Smart Set, it seems, can give points to them all

One reads of their deeds in the magazine article,
    Finds them exposed in the pamphlet and book;
Of virtue they seem to possess not a particle;
    None can be seen, though minutely you look.
Satirists rage, but their wit, which to hurt is meant,
    Somehow contrives to achieve the reverse;

Pleased and refreshed by the splendid advertisement,
    Straight they proceed to grow steadily worse.
Gibes, which their skin should pierce painfully through,
        tickle,
Such is the armour-clad state of their cuticle;
Minds such as theirs are but fitted to harbour a
Love for their meals and distaste for a Yarborough.
    These are a few of the things that are said
    In some of the papers and books I have read.

Oh, the scandals and sins of our modern society
Beat Greece and Rome in extent and variety;
Egypt and Babylon look very small,
The Smart Set, it seems, can give points to them all.

(*Enter* MR. W. T. STEAD *as the* GOOD FAIRY.)

THE GOOD FAIRY:

Whither, young lady, do you wander now?

LITTLE RED RIDING HOOD:

To see my Granny, Sir.

THE GOOD FAIRY:

Then I allow
That you do well; though truly there is danger
Within these glades of which the Wolf is Ranger.
But, tell me, if 'tis not a tiresome task,
What would you of good Mistress Grundy ask?

LITTLE RED RIDING HOOD:

Kind Sir, I have been asked by friends to dine,
Thereafter going to a pantomime,
And I would know if virtuous people may
Visit, unharmed, that form of Christmas play.

THE GOOD FAIRY:

A play! (*Thunder heard left.*)
A theatre! (*Thunder heard right.*)
What, a pantomime!
(*Thunder heard overhead.*)
Not while the stars which do above us shine
(When it is night); not while the balmy breeze
(When it is summer) agitates the trees;
Not while my pen, the source of all that's pure,
Can call a blessing on our brother Boer,
Will I consent to such an evil thing!
List to me, maiden, for I'm going to sing.

SONG: THE GOOD FAIRY.

I'm simply a fairy who's good.
I work on an excellent plan:
I show you concisely
The way to live wisely,
And help you whenever I can.
I point out the path that is straight,
And—chiefly—I do what I may
To give a peremptor-
y check to the tempter
Who wants you to go to his play.

For this is the maxim I strive to implant—
The theatre brings moral decay.
No matter how rigid a life you may lead,
You're lost if you go to a play.

Of Maeterlinck try to fight shy,
   Or greet him with booing and groans;
      Of Ibsen keep clear. Oh,
      Beware of Pinero,
   And shun the deplorable Jones.
Their motives are risky and wrong,
   Their heroines never quite nice;
      They eke out their follies
      With danceable dollies,
   And other creations of Vice.

They woo you with tragedy, lure you with farce,
They mingle the grave with the gay;
But turn a deaf ear and remember my words—
You're lost if you go to a play.

(Enter, with shrieks of laughter, the DEMONS, PINERO,
MAETERLINCK, JONES, *and* IBSEN.)

DEMONS *(all together)*:

Ha, ha, good maiden, listen not to one,
Ho, ho, who says the theatre you should shun.
He, he, his head reminds us of a bun.

GOOD FAIRY:

Their words suggest to me—as I'm a sinner—
A common corpse's phosphorescent shimmer.

DEMONS:

A thing you've said before,

QUARTETTE: DEMONS.

ALL:

We're four jolly dramatists
  Who write problem plays,
Entrancing the public
  In various ways;
Don't grudge the expense of it,
  But come round and see

IBSEN:

Your Ibsen,

MAETERLINCK:

  Your Maeterlinck,

PINERO:

Pinero,

JONES:

And me.

We aren't like those fellows who
  Make incomes like kings
By musical comedies
  And those sort of things.
Our aims are artistic,
  We don't write for pelf,

IBSEN:

Not Ibsen,

MAETERLINCK:

  Nor Maeterlinck,

PINERO:

Pinero,

JONES:

  Nor self.

Don't talk of your Barries or
  Your Marshalls and Hoods;
When it comes to play-writing,
  We're there with the goods.
Each critic our thorough
  Pre-eminence owns

IBSEN (*bowing*):

Of Ibsen,

MAETERLINCK (*bowing*):

  And Maeterlinck,

PINERO (*bowing*):
Pinero,

JONES (*bowing*):
And Jones.

GOOD FAIRY:

Avaunt, aroint thee! Aye, and out upon
You, decadent deceivers—get thee gone.
(*Drives out demons, who fly with derisive laughter.*)
And now, fair maiden, hence I quickly hie,
As I have several columns to supply
Ere half-past one. Yet though this demon crew
I have defeated, let me now anew
Warn you against a still more dreaded foe.
Mark well my words, that you at once may know
It when you see it. 'Tis a Wolf in guise,
With pleasant smile and most engaging eyes.
It pays no bills, yet is it finely dressed;
Or, if it pays, such payment is a test
Of its vulgarity and rich display,
And so you'd best avoid it either way.
At some fine restaurant it cannot fail
To lunch or dine, and in the *Daily Mail*
Records the fact. No Sunday can you fix
Whereon it plays not bridge from three to six,
Or races round upon a motor-car,
Till shrieking rustics know not where they are.
It uses slang, and never will it stick
At jokes which are as broad as they are thick.
'Tis Decadence complete, and life it fills
With all the very choicest moral ills.
Doth this appal you?

LITTLE RED RIDING HOOD:
Aye, in truth, good Sir,

GOOD FAIRY:

My best advice has often made a stir
In circles which are filled with honest men
Who love to read about the Upper Ten.
And so good-bye.
(GOOD FAIRY *flies off right.*)

(*Enter* SMART SET WOLF *in goggles and a motor-car.
He drives rapidly round the stage,* RED RIDING HOOD
*avoiding him with difficulty. Suddenly a loud explosion
is heard, and the car stops.*)

THE WOLF (*getting out*):

Would that I now could catch that addle-pater
Of a chauffeur, for my accelerator
Is never fast enough to suit my taste.
Ha! who is this?

LITTLE RED RIDING HOOD:

     A maiden, fair and chaste,
Who to substantial people can refer
If you desire from them a character.

THE WOLF:

Substantial folk! Mean you with money, child?

LITTLE RED RIDING HOOD:

Aye, Sir.

THE WOLF (*aside*):

    Ha, ha! then she must be beguiled
At once. The *nouveau riche* is Heaven sent
To those whose income is so quickly spent
As mine. Now, Smart Set, be a Wolf indeed,
Here is a morsel fit for *gourmet's* feed.
Come closer yet, my fascinating dear (*aloud*).

LITTLE RED RIDING HOOD:

Nay, Sir, excuse me, for I greatly fear
Whom you may be, and why a mask you wear.
I would prefer to see your features bare.

THE WOLF:

Nay, do not let my goggles cause alarm.
I'll sing to you; in that there's never harm.

SONG: THE SMART SET WOLF.

Oh! I am the king of a Social Ring
 Which nobody can define;
As bubbles pass to the rim of a glass
 When drinking your champagne wine,
As a lover's thrill or a "rendered" bill,
 So vague is this set of mine,
     Ha, ha!
 So vague is this set of mine.

If you like to be dressed in the Bond Street best,
 And pose as a social star,
If your heart is set on a landaulette
 Or a sixty-horse-power car,
Don't trouble to pay; it is never the way
 To pay in my set, ha, ha!
     Ha, ha!
 To pay in my set, Ha, Ha!

If you dance to the tune of Sir Francis Jeune
    And ·the Co. is a social pet,
Or tradesmen frown as you pass through town,
    And whisper of duns and debt,
Don't trouble, my dear, you've nothing to fear
    If you're in the Smart Smart Set,
                Ha, ha!
    One of my Smart Smart Set.

If your pretty face you would like to place
    In the illustrated press,
With a social par., saying who you are,
    And a sketch of your Ascot dress,
Your wish you will get if you join my set,
    For I am the thing, I guess,
                Ha, ha!
    The real, smart thing, I guess.

So come with me, on the strict Q.T.,
    To the pleasure world away,
Where nobody cares what a neighbour dares,
    And life is a funny play.
Where we jump and laugh round the Golden Calf,
    And everyone must be gay,
              Ha, ha!
    For that is the Smart Set way.

    (*Enter* GOOD FAIRY *on a sunbeam.*)

GOOD FAIRY:

It is the wolf; his goggles don't deceive me.
Ah, child, I was a careless chap to leave thee.

(*The* GOOD FAIRY *rushes at the* WOLF, *who flies to his motor-car and drives off in the direction of* MRS. GRUNDY'S *cottage.*)

    [QUICK CURTAIN.]

SCENE II.

The interior of MRS. GRUNDY'S *cottage. The* WOLF *is discovered disguised in a motor veil, and dressed in the fashion of the season before last, being the clothes of the grandmother,* MRS. GRUNDY, *whom he has just devoured. He is playing bridge at four o'clock on a Sunday afternoon because habit is too strong for him. Being alone, it is triple dummy; he is plainly bored. On the table are several bottles containing morphia, absinthe, crême de menthe, sal volatile, bay rum, and other exclusive drinks. French novels, theatre tickets, restaurant bills, post obits, bills of sale, and billets doux are scattered about the room. It is all very terrible.*

SONG : WOLF.

If you like a life of leisure,
    You should think before you go
In for unrestricted pleasure :
    It's the hardest work I know.
You must labour every second,
    Or your friends will soon forget
That you're anxious to be reckoned
    In the very smartest set.

You must worry Mrs. Grundy,
    And I'll tell you how it's done :
Bridge, especially on Sunday
    'Twixt the hours of ten and one;
Have your car too quickly driven,
    Have a biggish load of debt,
And a place you'll soon be given
    In the very smartest set.

But at times a thought steals o'er me,
    Spite of all that I can do,
That these rapid habits bore me :
    And I feel that it is true;
For one really can't help seeing
    In the people one has met,
Signs of weariness of being
    In the very smartest set.

Even Bridge, it is eternal,
    And distinctly apt to pall;
Indescribably infernal
    Is a motor, after all;
One grows tired of talking scandal,
    And, in short, you soon regret
That you thought it worth the candle
    To be in the smartest set.

(*Enter* LITTLE RED RIDING HOOD.)

LITTLE RED RIDING HOOD :

'Tis weary walking, and the Fairy good
Although he led me safely through the wood,
Such sound and wise advice did always pour
Into my ear, that he became a bore.
In truth, I could have wished, dear Grandmamma,
That I possessed a little motor-car,
Had I not known such wish was very wrong.
But look (*staring around in surprise*)—Dear Granny,
    you *are* going strong!
What! novels, absinthe, bridge, and on a Sunday!
Why, what will you be up to upon Monday?

THE WOLF :

My dear, I'm merely moving, like the *Times*,
We old folk must have pleasures.

DUET : LITTLE RED RIDING HOOD AND WOLF.

LITTLE RED RIDING HOOD :

I always used to think of you
As just a sober matron who
    Was eminently British.
But now, if I may candid be,
Upon my word, you seem to me,
    If anything, too skittish.
A cigarette with golden tip
Rests rakishly upon your lip :
I notice you are reading " Gyp,"
    That dangerous Parisian.
I see a pile of bills, unpaid,
And by your side, I'm much afraid,
A drink that isn't lemonade,
    Although it looks a fizzy 'un.
Oh, Grandmamma, explain to me
The meaning of the things I see.

THE WOLF :

When you grow up, you'll find that you
Must act as other people do,
    No matter what your will is.
That ancient saw has power yet—
Mutantur tempora, nos et
    Mutamur (change) *in illis.*
Now Fashion's curious decrees,
However much they may displease,
Are binding on her devotees;
    And so I answer truthfully,
That Fashion at the present day
Demands that, when your hair is grey,
You must behave in such a way
    As I am doing—youthfully.

And that, my child, appears to be
The meaning of the things you see.

LITTLE RED RIDING HOOD :

And this from you! Your sentiment in song
Convinces me the Fairy Good was wrong.
Then may I go and see the pantomime?

THE WOLF :

Of course, my duckling, we'll together dine,
And after take a box. I'll not forget
The opera glasses.

LITTLE RED RIDING HOOD :

Ah! I was so set
On going, that this news is one long joy;
Hurray for mirth, and banish all annoy.

THE WOLF :

Embrace me, sweet one.

(The WOLF is just about to eat up LITTLE RED RIDING HOOD, when a great noise is heard without. The door is burst open, and the GOOD FAIRY appears, uttering loud hunting cries, and blowing his own trumpet. He is followed by the HUNTERS, represented by MESSRS. BENSON, R. J. CAMPBELL, SUTRO, and MESDAMES CORELLI and "RITA." The HUNTERS form an effective group, facing the audience. As there is no room for the GOOD FAIRY he stands on a chair behind them, trying to attract attention by waving his arms. The WOLF, after watching them for a time, walks out of the door and does not return.)

HUNTERS' CHORUS.

MARIE CORELLI :

I write, exposing wealthy folk,
Who think the Sabbath day a joke;
  I castigate the nobly-born
  Who don't " behave as sich."
I earn a large emolument
By volume after volume, meant
  To institute a series of reforms among the rich.

CHORUS :

And our efforts, we believe, 'll soon eradicate
  the evil;
  We shall deal it a demoralising blow:
Oh, we mean to crush the Smart Set,
On destroying it our heart's set;
  For it's really quite too shocking, don't you
  know.

ALFRED SUTRO :

You've seen " The Walls of Jericho,"
In which I do my best to show
   That customs in Belgravia,
   Are, to put it mildly, odd.
Birth? Breeding? Pah! I flout it all,
And prove beyond a doubt at all,
   That a miner who has money is the noblest work
      of God.

REV. R. J. CAMPBELL :

Within the pulpit, week by week,
I'm generally heard to speak
   Of horrifying goings-on
   That mar the gay week-end.
I hate the conduct such as is
The wont of dukes and duchesses,
   When staying at the truly rural mansion of a
      friend.

RITA :

I spend my time in trying to teach
The upper classes decent speech ;
   For slanginess of every sort
   I resolutely ban.
I shudder at their riskiness ;
They speak of " twee " and " diskiness,"
   And talk about their " nighties," and I wonder how
      they *can!*

E. F. BENSON :

I'm not the sort of chappie, what ?
To bar a man because he's got
   An income much too big for him ;
   I only hate display.
It makes a chap despise it so
To see them advertise it so,
   In just that beastly vulgah sort of Yankee kind
      of way.

CHORUS :

   And our efforts, we believe, 'll soon eradicate
      the evil ;
   We shall deal it a demoralising blow :
Yes, we mean to crush the Smart Set,
On destroying it our heart's set ;
   For it's really quite too shocking, don't you
      know.

THE HUNTERS (*together*) :

Now for the Wolf; stamp, slay, and eke destroy
This hardened wretch, this incomplete alloy
Of vice, extravagance, and vulgar show.
Hello, he's gone!   Did you, sir, see him go?
             (*To the* GOOD FAIRY.)

GOOD FAIRY:

Not I. It was your business. Though I own
That I should miss him if instead of flown
He now were dead. For what on earth should I
Have left to write about? Morality
Will ne'er provide a column, while a crime
Fills twenty pages. Therefore make no fuss.

THE HUNTERS (*together*):

Good for the Fairy! So say all of us.

GOOD FAIRY (*to* LITTLE RED RIDING HOOD):

We've held the stage enough. And what may you,
If I dare make so bold, intend to do?
Will you come back with me?

LITTLE RED RIDING HOOD:

I tell you, no:
I find your conversation very slow.

GOOD FAIRY *and* HUNTERS (*together*):

Then will you join the Wolf? Will you become
A member of the Smart Set? We are done
Entirely, if such dreadful infamy
You choose. Will you go visiting a play
The product of a wicked demon's brain?
From such ignoble conduct pray refrain.

LITTLE RED RIDING HOOD:

A play! We're at one now.

GOOD FAIRY:

Alas! she's mad,
Or else entirely going to the bad.

LITTLE RED RIDING HOOD:

A play, I say, and eke a problem play,
Is what we all are acting in to-day.

GOOD FAIRY:

Explain, poor child.

LITTLE RED RIDING HOOD:

Then, prithee, tell me now,
Am I about to join the Wolf or vow
To tread the virtuous path whereon we pass
Our lives—we of the Upper Middle Class?

GOOD FAIRY:

That is a problem that I do not know.

LITTLE RED RIDING HOOD:

Forgive me if I say I told you so.
It is a problem. Therefore fairly may
We dub this little piece a *Problem Play.*

THE REST:

Ah, horror!

> (*From without is heard the howl of a Wolf.
> The* GOOD FAIRY *flies up the chimney.
> The* HUNTERS *cluster together as the
> curtain falls.*)

A WINTER'S TALE
KING ARTHUR & HIS COURT

'*VANITY FAIR*'
14TH DECEMBER 1905

A WINTER'S TALE.

KING ARTHUR AND HIS COURT.

DRAMATIS PERSONÆ.

King Arthur's Court.

King Arthur .... MR. A. J. BALFOUR.
Queen Guinevere .... THE UNIONIST PARTY.
Sir Lancelot...................... THE TARIFF REFORM LEAGUE.
Merlin (*out of a job*) .... THE DUKE OF DEVONSHIRE.
Sir Kaye .... THE MARQUIS OF LONDONDERRY.
Free Fooders, Retaliators, Tariff Reformers, and other retainers.

Barbarians.

Sir Campbell (*a noted Scot*) ...... SIR H. CAMPBELL-BANNERMAN.
Sir Primrose (*a cultivated Pict*)... THE EARL OF ROSEBERY.
Sir Lloyd (*a Cymric*)............... MR. LLOYD-GEORGE.
Sir Redmond (*The Irish Chief*) MR. REDMOND.
Sir Grey (*a patriotic Goth*) ...... SIR EDWARD GREY.
Sir Keir (*an advanced Hun*)...... MR. KEIR HARDIE.
Sir Winston (*a conspirator*) ...... MR. WINSTON CHURCHILL.

Passive Resisters, Anti-Vaccinators, Members of the Humanitarian League, Contributors to *The Daily News*, Members of the National Liberal Club, and other retainers.

ACT I.

(*A forest near* KING ARTHUR'S *Castle. On the right, upon a grassy mound,* SIR PRIMROSE *is discovered unarmed, clothed in white samite, crowned with flowers, and solacing his solitude upon a viol. In the centre is an open glade, giving a distant view of* KING ARTHUR'S *Castle, yclept "Ye Government," which is surrounded by the tents of the Barbarian Army, consisting of Picts, Scots, Rads, Cymrics, Celts, and other outlandish tribes who are besieging it. To the left is a perspective of tree-trunks.*)

SIR PRIMROSE:

There may be some in yon outlandish host
(Who once, upraising me on lifted shields,
Proclaimed me Leader) that declare me base,
Neglectful of my party and my cause,
Neglectful of my chance to trip the heels
Of Arthur in his day of trial sore.
Yet how can I, a cultivated man,
A perfect stylist and a connoisseur,
A critic, too, a student of the men
Who made the nations, stoop to join a band
Of rebel Irish, Welshmen from the hills,

26

Rads from Londinium, Picts from mine own land?
Such men, forsooth, as would disjoin the kingdoms,
In peace I will remain, apart from strife,
Forgetting care in music:—

SONG: SIR PRIMROSE.

The political arena was at one time just as clean a
    Place as anyone could ever wish to see;
But it's suffered changes lately: it's deteriorated greatly
    Till it's really quite unsuitable for me.
Oh, the chatter and the babble of this unimperial rabble
    Is more than a philosopher can bear,
So, although it has annoyed them, I consistently avoid them,
    For politics are nothing like they were.

When the trumpet sounds for action there is much dissatisfaction
    (Which they seldom try their hardest to conceal)
For, instead of keenly leaping to the conflict, I am sleeping,
    Quite oblivious to their passionate appeal.
There are some who say I'm skulking; not a few who call it sulking;
    But for trifles such as these I do not care:
At the cost of irritation I preserve my isolation,
    For politics are nothing like they were.

I can hear the din and rattle of an energetic battle,
    I can hear the shouts of stormers at the breach;
But it seems at such a distance that I don't provide assistance
    (With the possible exception of a speech).
In a gentlemanly manner, as they rally round the banner,
    I recommend the troops to do and dare;
But of course I never heed them when they shout to me to lead them,
    For politics are nothing like they were.

In the good old days when I myself was fighting
    We did things in a cultured sort of style;
We made the fray sufficiently exciting,
    But stuck to flag and Empire all the while.
We hadn't any faction in our army,
    By discipline each warrior was tied:
But the state of things at present is so thoroughly unpleasant
    That I think it best to stay away outside.

    (*A drum heard without. Enter the Barbarian
    Army of Rads, Celts, Cymrics, &c., preceded by
    large banners, after the fashion of a Trade
    Union demonstration.*)

MARCHING SONG OF BARBARIAN ARMY.

THE ARMY (*all together*):

A host with but a single aim
    We fight in perfect unity;
No foe upon the earth can claim
    To treat us with impunity:
Each man regards the others
As something more than brothers.

The enemy don't relish it
When we detect his whereabouts.
We never have a jar or split,
We're always chums (or thereabouts);
In fair and stormy weather
We always march together.

SIR GREY (*leading detachment of Respectable Imperial Liberals*):

Our loyalty's free from defect,
Our morals are highly correct;
We put down our foot
On proposals to loot,
For Property's rights we respect.
We stick with a firmness intense
To Imperial views (which are Sense).
Whatever we pay
We must lead the way:
Our motto is "*Blow* the expense!"

SIR LLOYD (*leading detachment of earnest and advanced Rads*):

We act on a different plan,
Imperial notions we ban:
When the foe we defeat
Both the army and fleet
We propose to cut down (if we can).
With shrewd, economical glance
We watch o'er affairs of finance,
We've a wonderful sense
For the value of pence,
And save them whene'er we've a chance.

SIR KEIR (*leading detachment of Unemployed*):

We cawn't siy we 'olds very much
With these aristocratics and such.
The pore son of toil
'As a right to the spoil;
We sticks to wotever we touch.
Wot we ses is, this Chivalry's rot,
Let's beat 'em, and tike orl they've got.
Let the 'ard-working man
Gavver orl that he can,
And not 'ave no scruples. Thet's wot.

SIR REDMOND (*leading detachment of "pure-minded" Celts*):

Ah, shtop all this terruble noise!
Go aisy, that's what I advoise:
For it's little we heed
If we fail or succeed;
Bedad, it's all wan to the bhoys.
We don't care which side we assist.
Is ut upset the Monarchy? Whist!
We'll just march with the host
Which'll pay us the most:
Them's our sintiments, nately exprissed.

*(The Barbarian Army march round the stage, and
then line up left and right. The leaders gather
in the centre to welcome that gentle Knight,
SIR CAMPBELL, who advances on foot, followed
by a drummer carrying the Party drum.)*

SIR CAMPBELL:

Fair and dear friends, right strongly did you sing,
And though I noticed, scattered here and there,
A note that broke the general consonance;
Yet on the whole the noise was very great,
And doubtless will affright the knights that laze
About the Table Round within the Castle
Of proud King Arthur (where I shortly hope
We shall be dining). Yet in common cause
Must we be bound, with single heart and hand
Must we strike home if victory is to gild
Our spreading pinions. Firstly let us storm
The castle walls; hereafter can we heal
The little rifts that in the Party lute
Now threaten discords.

(SIR GREY *steps forward.*)
Ah, my lusty knight,
What have you for your leader's longing ears?

SIR GREY:

My gentle leader. Though I would not loose
The dogs of dark contention, yet Sir Redmond
And I have had some bickerings on the way.
May not the army pause the while I thrust
His black opinions down his baneful throat?

SIR PRIMROSE (*descending the mound, and entering the*
arena):

Alas! my comrades,
It seems to me that I must make a speech.

Sir Lloyd and Sir Keir:

Nay, let *us* speak.

Sir Campbell:

Now drummer haste and do your noisy duty.
(*A long and thunderous roll on the Party drum
drowns the turmoil. As it, at last, concludes
Sir Campbell steps forward.*)

Song : Sir Campbell.

When my party's every action
Tends to drive me to distraction
    And affairs begin to hum,
    I beat my drum.
When they call for an effective
And immediate corrective
    Then I play, until they're dumb
    Upon the drum.

It doesn't matter much about the meaning or the air,
So long as I play something people never seem to care,
I initiate a panic or alleviate a scare
    With my drum.

I've reduced it to a science:
When the foemen shriek defiance
    And my army's looking glum,
    I beat my drum.
When my party in a fix is,
All at sevens and at sixes,
    To reorganise the scrum
    I beat the drum.

It is simply sound and fury, and it's meaning isn't clear,
But I fancy it encourages my men to persevere;
So I still continue playing, though the enemy may sneer,
    On the drum.

So my tip to young tacticians,
If they get in tight positions
    And the prospect's rather rum,
    Is "Beat the drum."
For the squabblings and the hootings
And the brawlings and disputings
    May be neatly overcome
    With the drum.

Dissension in your forces it infallibly destroys,
It soothes your own supporters, while the foemen it annoys;
Don't try to play a tune: you only need a lot of noise
    From the drum.

Sir Primrose:

And this is leadership! Now Heaven defend
The shrieking rabble and their captain, who
Is but a drummer—save the Yankee term—
But, hist, whom have we here?

(*Enter* Sir Winston *and friends, carrying a white flag.*)

        Now, can it be
They are a sub-committee of surrender?

Sir Winston :

My friends, I bid you greeting. We have fled
From Arthur's Castle, which can never be
A home again—save chance should spin around
Her mocking wheel. For in its splendid halls
Is dire confusion. 'Neath King Arthur's nose
Does Lancelot make eyes at Guinevere.
So that the lady sits in dire distress,
Not knowing what is what nor who is who.
And while the knights with gossip fill the days
There's none that pays attention to our claims
To high advancement, none that are so poor
To do us reverence, to observe our words;
Write of us in the papers—to be brief,
We are neglected, treated, sirs, like boys.
So here we are, your fond and keen allies.
Hark, for I much desire to sing to you.

Song : Sir Winston.

From my childhood I've nourished ambition,
 I made up my mind in my cot
To climb to the highest position,
 Whether people approved me or not.
So I cut some remarkable capers,
 Went out with the army to war,
And wrote myself up in the papers :
 (That's all that the papers are for.)

With Arthur I next was connected,
 For Arthur was then in his prime :
When greybeards in council collected,
 I gave them advice every time.
A youth who's determined to preach is
 Regarded, I know, as a bore,
But I got myself known by my speeches :
 (That's all that my speeches were for.)

For months with allegiance unaltered
 I stuck to him closer than glue;
Nor ever in battle I faltered;
 I fought with the vigour of two.
No fierce opposition dismayed me,
 I yearned to be shedding my gore;
I fancied that loyalty paid me :
 (That's all that my loyalty's for.)

But my monarch is now a back number,
He seems to be quite up a tree,
And Arthur can only encumber
A pushing young fellow like me.
So, though it's a bit of a gamble,
I fancy I stand to gain more
If I throw in my lot with Sir Campbell:
(That's all that Sir Campbell is for.)

SIR CAMPBELL:

Your words sound strangely to my simple ears.

SIR LLOYD:

Strange bedfellows does Opposition bring.

SIR REDMOND:

Silence, ye grumblers.   Does he know a way
To storm the castle, plant our banner proud
Upon the inner wall?

SIR WINSTON:

In truth I do.

SIR REDMOND:

Expound, my gentle sir.

SIR WINSTON:

Appoint me leader
And you shall win the day without a doubt.

(*Intense and prolonged uproar.   Finally,* SIR
CAMPBELL *calls upon the Party drum to do its
duty.   Silence is at last restored.*)

SIR CAMPBELL:

Patience, young man.   The steps to office high
Are steep and many.   In some thirty years
You may, perchance, I say you may, perhaps,
Attain some small emolument.   Enough.
A flank attack is what we now intend
On our disordered foes.   Come, forward, march,
Advance our banners, let the policeman clear
A way for this, our army.   Victory waits
To crown us as we storm the Castle gates.

(*Exeunt, singing* " *A host with but a single aim.*")

32

ACT II.

(Midnight; Moonlight.—SIR LANCELOT (*the Tariff Reform League*) *is discovered with guitar beneath the window of* GUINEVERE (*the Unionist Party*). *In a neighbouring corner of the battlements a group of Free Fooders, headed by* MERLIN (*the* DUKE OF DEVONSHIRE), *are watching him.*)

SIR LANCELOT (*the Tariff Reform League*):

> Of dear little parties on earth,
>   No dearth,
> I've noted; they've not been a few.
> Their charms I do not underrate,
>   They're great.
> But they can't hold a candle to you,
>   To you.
> They can't hold a candle to you.

> Can you hear,
> Guinevere,
>   What I'm saying, my dear?
> Your window is open, besides being near.
> Can you hear?

CHORUS OF FREE FOODERS (*ironically*):

> Hear! hear!

SIR LANCELOT:

> Can you hear?

CHORUS OF FREE FOODERS:

> Oh, Lancelot, oh, Lancelot,
> Your captivating glance a lot
>   Of damage has effected, it is clear.
> It's a puzzle what she sees
> In your visage that can please,
>   But the fact remains, you wheedle Guinevere.

SIR LANCELOT:

> Can you hear?

CHORUS OF FREE FOODERS:

> Oh, Lancelot, oh, Lancelot,
> In gay and giddy France a lot
>   Of people act like this, but still it's queer
> That in England you should seek
> In this shameful way to speak.
>   Please remember she's King Arthur's Guinevere.

(GUINEVERE (*the Unionist Party*) *appears at the window.*)

GUINEVERE :

>As fast asleep just now I lay,
>   Asleep and gently dreaming,
>I thought I heard, far, far away,
>   The sound of someone screaming.
>It may have been the nightingales·
>   Those shrill, nocturnal gurglers,
>Just practising their notes and scales.
>   Or possibly it's burglars.

(She sees LANCELOT.*)*

>Oh, Lancelot! You there! What next!
>You know that Arthur would be vexed.

SIR LANCELOT :

>Yes, yes, 'tis I. I know it's wrong.
>   But how could I resist it ?
>A brief synopsis of my song
>   I'll give you as you missed it.
>In (though I say it) neatish verse
>   I told the love I bore you.
>Oh, Guinevere, my doubt disperse;
>   You know that I adore you.

GUINEVERE :

>The blood to my embarrassed cheek
>   With sudden quickness rushes :
>Look close if you my answer seek;
>   You'll read it in my blushes.
>I know the vows you make are true,
>   All other kinds are spurious :
>I'd like to run away with you,
>   But Arthur would be *furious.*

SIR LANCELOT :

>Nay, hear me, Guinevere, your heart
>   No worn-out bonds must fetter :
>We've got to make another start,
>   The sooner done, the better.
>For ancient shibboleths who cares?
>   Our lives they must not tether :
>And we must manage our affairs
>   On new lines altogether.

CHORUS OF FREE FOODERS :

>Oh Lancelot, oh, Lancelot,
>We stamp our feet, and dance a lot
>   With rage and disapproval when we hear
>The matrimonial change
>Which you callously arrange
>   For your poor, misguided victim, Guinevere.

SIR KAYE (*the* MARQUIS OF LONDONDERRY), *rushing violently in, and speaking in recitative*) :

>Ha! What is this! Beneath the Royal window
>I see a man.

(Exit Sir Lancelot *by rope. They all rush forward, and stand shaking their heads sadly.)*

ACT III.

(The interior of King Arthur's *Castle, "Ye Govern-
ment." In the centre at back of stage is a dais, on which
are placed two thrones, in the occupation of* King Arthur
(Mr. A. J. Balfour) *and* Guinevere *(the Unionist Party).
Behind them are grouped* Sir Lancelot, Sir Kaye (Lord
Londonderry), *and other officials. Below the dais is the
Round Table, at which a number of knights are seated.*

King Arthur :

My comrades, we have heard without our walls
Rumour of strife in the Barbarian hordes
That think to pillage this, our citadel,
Where we for many years have held our court
Despite the flouts and sneers of evil men.
Let us be careful not to emulate
Their rude alarms and indiscreet excursions,
I ask you then to fill your beakers up
And drink to this our Cause.

> *(The assembly rise to their feet with much
> cheering.)*

A Voice :   What cause?

King Arthur *(in great annoyance)*:
What knight is this who breaks the general joy
With such a question? 'Tis enough, we know
Each in our hearts what is—what is our Cause.

Guinevere :

Dear Arthur, now for many loving years
Have I obeyed you, followed every move,
Accepted explanations, borne myself
As should a true and virtuous British matron.
Yet even I would rather like to know,
Being perplexed by doubts and general fears,
What is the Cause for which we fight to-day.

King Arthur :
You, too, my Guinevere !

35

Song: King Arthur.

Oh, the life of a king is not skittles and beer at all;
   Worries pursue him wherever he flies,
Chase him, and face him, and won't disappear at all,
   Worries! He's in them right up to the eyes.
Everyone seems to delight in perplexing him,
   Asking him questions he can't understand,
Boring and heckling and teasing and vexing him,
   Making him show all the cards in his hand,
Robbing his brain of all snap and lucidity,
Bleaching his locks with a frightful rapidity,
Into his confidence artfully burrowing,
Giving him shocks till his forehead is furrowing,
   Threatening mutiny every day—
   That is his subjects' unvarying way.

  How can a monarch preserve his urbanity,
  Feeling himself on the verge of insanity?
  Common folk grumble, and that sort of thing,
  But their woes can't compare with the woes of a king.

Oh! *vitæ* (to quote from the Classical) *tædia!*
   Life (to translate) is a poor sort of show.
Treated, by gad! as an Encyclopædia,
   All things on earth I'm expected to know.
I've got to answer with unimpaired bonhomie
   Questions of every kind they may ask:
Posers abstruse on the nation's Economy—
   That's but a tithe, so to speak, of my task.
Where are our Army Corps? Can I confirm any
   Rumours of war with the Sultan or Germany?
Are the Chinese on the Rand flogged diurnally?
Why should the Straphanger suffer eternally?
   Do the "All Blacks" play quite fair in the scrum?
   Daily the questions continue to come.

  How can a monarch go beaming with cheerfulness,
  When in a state that's approaching to tearfulness?
  Common folk grumble, and that sort of thing,
  But the man who is really oppressed is the king.

A Messenger (*rushing in*):

Arm, arm! The enemy have climbed the wall.

   (*A confused noise without. Shouts, alarums, and
   cheap excursions. Headed by* Sir Campbell,
   *the Barbarians rush into the hall. The Knights
   of the Round Table draw their swords and
   gather round the dais.*)

Sir Campbell:

  We ask

Sir Primrose:
    suggest,
Sir Keir,
      insist,

Sir Redmond:
        demand that you

ALL TOGETHER:

Deliver up this castle to our powers.

KING ARTHUR:

Nay, gentlemen, I charge you, tell me this,
Whom must I answer, who, in short, is chief?

SIR CAMPBELL:

I, by the sanction of the general voice.
Of all the Rads throughout my territories.

SIR KAYE:

Oh, my Royal King,
Whose words have ever been to me as laws,
Whose arguments are mine, whose thoughts are
mine,
I beg you———

KING ARTHUR:

Pray you, give me leave to speak.
These interruptions are mal apropos.

DUET: SIR CAMPBELL AND KING ARTHUR.

SIR C.:

Misfortune's dogged me from the first,
As you may plainly see:
Of luckless men I am the worst—

KING A. (aside):

You are, excepting me.

SIR C.:

My troops cause endless toil before
I get them into line,
And when I do, there's civil war—

KING A. (aside):

It's just the same with mine.

SIR C.:

They start at early morning, and
They quarrel all the day;
With "Traitor!" they each other brand—

KING A. (aside):

That's just what my men say.

SIR C.:

Their reverence for my words is small,
We always disagree:
They say I'm not their chief at all—

KING A. (aside):

Some say the same of me!

KING ARTHUR:

Sir Campbell, we'll adjourn this conference.
To you I leave this castle, on the plain.
We'll presently conjoin in battle dire,
So shall we know who's master, if it be
That any man can ever know who's master.

(*Exit* KING ARTHUR, *leading the way from the
Castle of* "*Ye Government.*" GUINEVERE
follows on the arm of SIR LANCELOT, *with*
MERLIN *and* SIR KAYE *gloomily regarding
them. As the curtain falls the Barbarians
have fallen to fighting desperately amongst
themselves, and* SIR CAMPBELL *is calling for
the Party drum.*)

B. FLETCHER ROBINSON.
P. G. WODEHOUSE.

THE PROGRESSIVE'S PROGRESS

SOME MEMORIES OF 1906

'THE WORLD'

1ST JANUARY 1907

THE PROGRESSIVE'S PROGRESS;
SOME MEMORIES OF 1906.

SCENE I.

Old Palace Yard, Westminster. Time, five o'clock in the afternoon. Enter M. Pierre Bonhomme, a Paris Municipal Councillor, personally conducted by Mr. Will Spender, M.P., L.C.C., a prominent and most progressive Wastrel.

M. BONHOMME. And this, Sir Spender, is your House of Commons, the home of British liberty upon which the sun nevare sets. I rejoice myself at this spectacle, so magnificent.

MR. SPENDER (*in his best platform manner*). I do not hesitate to say, Mossoo, that the House of Commons, garrisoned—if I may so express myself, though a hater of the military—with Radicals, Labour Members, and the flower of the London County Council, is a unique object in our history.

M. BONHOMME. Nobly said, Sir Spender. But tell me, Monsieur, is it true that which we hear, that your country, so beautiful, rejoices in her bold fraternal Government, and that your town, so great, has taken the London County Council to its heart? In short, is it that all are satisfied in England?

MR. SPENDER (*boldly*). I answer in the affirmative with no uncertain voice. The Progressive Party, for example, arouses a wild enthusiasm among every class in the citizen community which—er—which hopes to make anything out of it. Peace, Prosperity, and Progress is our motto; which we will obtain, regardless, I repeat, regardless of expense.

Song.—MR. WILLIAM SPENDER, M.P., L.C.C.

When I tell you, Mossoo,
What in London we do,
You'll be filled with a sudden surprise,
Not a city, I know,
Has such vigour and go;
I think we shall open your eyes.

For our Office of Works
No expense ever shirks,
And we pay all our men double wage,
Though we're millions in debt,
Do we trouble or fret?
Not a bit; we just move with the age.

On the river our Fleet
Is progressive and neat,
Though no passengers there you may see,
I would have you to note
That the crews have a vote ;
And that is sufficient for me.

But enough—here one turns
To the thought of John Burns
And Keir Hardie, our Government's lord,
They'll back any project,
For money's no object,
If Labour will only applaud.

M. Bonhomme. Ideal, generous people ! In my country they would
be so base as to consider the cost. But who is this who now approaches ?

[*Enter Policeman A 1, who marches sadly into the centre of the
stage and stands immersed in gloom. Presently he commences
to sing.*

Song.—Policeman A 1.

When I was but a lad, I told my father
I meant to join the Force. Did he approve ?
He shook his head, as if he thought this rather
A rash and injudicious kind of move.
" My boy," he answered, " you shall have your will, but
I fear that you will find, before you've done,
How true is that remark of Mr. Gilbert,
' A pleeceman's lot is not a happy one.' "

I'm one, you know, as modest as they make 'em,
With women I am diffident and shy :
Around the waist I never wish to take 'em,
I sort of rather blushes when they're by.
Yet Suffragettes a-raising a commotion,
I have to hug quite closely, or they run,
It's dooty, simply dooty—*not* devotion,
A pleeceman's lot is not a happy one.

I'm one, you know, though not exactly snobby,
Wot 'as an eye, I *must* say, for a gent ;
I hold it's most degrading for a bobby
To touch his hat to this here Parliament.
These Labour Members ! Lor', they're what you meet with
When you are out and have forgot your gun :
Not one as I'd be seen to cross the street with,
A pleeceman's lot is not a happy one.

39

I'm what you'd call an anything-for-peace man ;
   That's why you see this frown upon my face.
Lor', lumme, it's no joke to be a pleeceman
   In this here present blooming year of grace.
I'm hustled and I'm harassed and I'm flurried :
   And 'ave I any compensations? None!
I'm trod on, I'm " commissioned," and I'm worried.
   A pleeceman's lot is not a happy one.

M. BONHOMME. All is betrayed! Did you not hear his sentiments ?
Do you not perceive that he is an aristocrat in disguise ?

MR. SPENDER. You are mistaken. He was born in Battersea.

M. BONHOMME. But I thought you said that all the lower classes
welcomed the advent of Labour to——

MR. SPENDER. Hush ! Pardon me, Mossoo, if I take cover behind
you.

   [*He falls upon his hands and knees. After a minute he rises,
     looking uneasily about him.*

MR. SPENDER. Forgive me, but I thought I heard Suffragettes. We
are all terrified of 'em ; especially the Prime Minister.

               [*Enter Peers, marching in fours (right)*.

               Chorus of Peers.

The saviours of the country, we !
No finer statesmen you will see.
Rely upon your House of Peers
(So long as no one interferes)
To put all difficulties right,
If we have to sit up all the night
   To do it, to do it.

We don't mind owning that, perhaps,
We once were sleepy sort of chaps.
We must confess we liked to doze :
Our state was rather comatose.
But now we show an iron will ;
Remember Mr. Birrell's Bill !
   We slew it ! we slew it !

No finer statesmen you will see :
The saviours of the country, we !

[Enter Radical Members of Parliament, marching in pairs (left).
Chorus of Radical M.P.s.

The saviours of the country, we!
No finer statesmen you will see.
Our blood's not very blue, we know ;
But when it comes to brains, what ho !
You will not find our names in Burke,
But if you ask for honest work,
We do it, we do it.

We don't mind owning, now and then
We have our rows, like other men.
But if sometimes we disagree—
Well, well, these things have got to be !
Why talk about these small upsets ?
The subject's painful, so don't let's
Pursue it, pursue it.

No finer statesmen you will see :
The saviours of the country, we.

M. Bonhomme. How boldly do the aristocrats address the noble Radicals ! Have you no lanterns in London ?

Mr. Spender. Magic lanterns ?

M. Bonhomme (*darkly*). To hang a man upon. It is most true that the earth would be glorious without these wicked men. No bishops, no religion, no army, no navy, no sport, no——

Mr. Spender (*hastily*). Of course, of course. At the same time it would make no difference to the Nonconformists. When you say " No religion," you mean " No Established Church."

M. Bonhomme. Not at all. We Radicals of France are against all religions. We are humanists, cosmopolitans. Down with all churches, chapels, seminaries !——

Mr. Spender. I say, Mossoo, steady on. If Dr. Clifford were to hear you ! Or R. J. Campbell !

M. Bonhomme. Pish ! You are no true Democrat !

Mr. Spender (*uneasily*). We must go slowly, Mossoo. We must move step by step. But, hush ! Here comes the Premier.

[Enter Sir H. C.-B., in Privy Councillor's uniform, to a flourish
of drums and trumpets. At his right hand advance certain
Labour Members in the full dress of British Non-Working Men.
As the Premier steps forward, they also advance.

Song.—THE PREMIER (*with interruptions*).

PREMIER.   I'm Premier of this mighty land,
            And none dispute my sway;
(LABOUR MEM. That's all his fun, you understand;
            We do it every day.)
PREMIER.   Men rush to do my will; and woe
            Betide 'em if they're tardy!
(LAB. MEM. That's just his little joke, you know:
            He grovels to Keir Hardie.)
PREMIER.   I'm monarch wheresoe'er I go!
(LAB. MEM. He *grovels* to Keir Hardie.)

PREMIER.   Oh, great reforms I'll carry out,
            With no delay or fuss.
(LAB. MEM. He'd like to try it on, no doubt,
            But daren't, because of us.)
PREMIER.   Just watch them quail when I begin,
            Like Jove, to wield the thunder.
(LAB. MEM. Of course, all that is rather thin,
            We always keep him under.)
PREMIER.   My iron will is bound to win!
(LAB. MEM. *We* make him knuckle under.)

POLICEMAN A 1 (*entering right*). Beg your pardin, Sir Henry, but the Suffragettes——
[*The Premier flies, followed by the Radical and Labour Members, amid cries of alarm.*

M. BONHOMME (*wildly*). I do not comprehend. The Radicals they command the Conservatives, and the Premier commands the Radicals, and the Labour members command the Premier, and the Suffragettes they——

MR. SPENDER (*hastily*). Come, sir, let us on.

(*Curtain.*)

SCENE II.

Hyde Park in the neighbourhood of the Reformers' Tree. Time: midday. Enter M. Bonhomme and Mr. Spender.

M. BONHOMME. And I have seen the—the—"exercise ground of Society"? Is that not so?

MR. SPENDER (*solemnly*). Here walk the bloated millionaire and the proud duchess, surrounded by their crawling sycophants. Here swaggers the dissolute peer with whose infamies all England desires to be familiar.

M. BONHOMME. And who is he?

MR. SPENDER. Practically any peer.

42

M. Bonhomme (*cheerfully*). Ah! the young blood! Even we social-istic-republicans in Paris——

Mr. Spender. I don't want to know about Paris. In this country it is understood that all peers are dissolute and all members of the labouring classes are temperate and pure. I beg you not to attack that theory, if you love liberty.

M. Bonhomme. And why?

Mr. Spender. Well—er—you see, all our policy is based upon it. It is understood that a working man is so honest that he can be trusted to spend thousands of pounds upon the Borough Councils, or hundreds of thousands upon the County Councils, or millions in the House of Commons. All waste, wife-beating, infidelity, peculation, immorality, and mismanagement belong to the aristocracy—by right, as it were.

M. Bonhomme. You surprise me! Yet it is understandable. For me, I hate the aristocrats.

Mr. Spender. Here comes a desperate scoundrel.

M. Bonhomme. But how do you know?

Mr. Spender. He is a peer. I have seen his photo in the *Church Times*.

[*Enter Peer, a little man with a flannel collar, pince-nez, and a weary air.*

Song: "*The Respectable Peer.*"

I'm not a bad fellow at heart;
  I'm kind and well-meaning, I think.
    But, despite all my labours,
    My friends and my neighbours
  Consider me blacker than ink.
In the set that is flashy and smart
  My innocent self they enroll;
    They scoff and they sneer
    At the view that a Peer
  May combine with his title a soul.

They murmur, "Take care! He's a Peer!
They say he's ten thousand a year!
    Run and fetch Father Vaughan
    To pour buckets of scorn
On the head of this dissolute Peer!"

To church every Sunday I go,
(Yes, even on rainy days), twice.
Their comments are bitter :
" Transparent ! " they titter,
" Hypocrisy cannot cloak vice."
The Park I find dreary and slow,
And so, as a rule, stop away.
My absence is noted,
They think I have moted
To Brighton, perhaps, for the day.

They murmur, " Ah, just like a Peer !
In his car on a Sunday. Dear, dear !
Let us hope the police
Will soon cause to decrease
The joy of this dissolute Peer ! "

Plain water I take at my meals :
I don't like French cooking at all.
But the Radical presses
Denounce my excesses
In a manner designed to appal.
My name in connection with " deals "
Of the shadier sort you won't see.
But each man shakes his head
At the stories he's read,
And thinks what my profits can be.

They murmur : " Take care, he's a Peer !
His ways are decidedly queer.
His transactions on 'Change
Are—well, let us say, strange.
He's a thoroughly rascally Peer."

M. BONHOMME. Poor fellow ! his lot is sad.

MR. SPENDER. But he is a peer.

M. BONHOMME. Sir Spender, we democrats in France recognise no class distinctions. I do not care whether he is a duke or a gamin of the streets. I say I am sorry for him.

MR. SPENDER (gloomily). That's not the right way to look at things. All our Labour members——

M. BONHOMME. Have met him, and found cause to dislike him, hein ?

MR. SPENDER. No ; but they've *read* about peers in *Reynolds's*.

M. BONHOMME. Please do not be so foolish. That is no true democratic talk. But tell me who are these—so sad, so disconsolate ?

[*Enter a small and ragged body of the Unemployed.*

44

Chorus of Unemployed.

It ain't a bit o' use, you know,
    Us trying to look cheerful ;
We're out of jobs, you see.   What ho !
    I tell you straight, it's fearful.
The way the working man's oppressed,
And kicked, and trod on, and the rest,
    Is simply something fearful.

Work makes us ill, there ain't a doubt.
    The very thought of wheeling
A barrowful of bricks about
    Gives us that tired feeling.
Whenever we are asked to plod
Up ladders, carrying a hod,
    We get that tired feeling.

We like our pipes, we like our drink
    (At that there ain't no shirking),
We like to lie in bed and think
    Of other fellows working,
We lie awake in bed and shake
With 'earty laughter till we ache
    Through thinkin' how they're working.

But still the pineful fact remains
    That no one will employ us ;
It looks as though they racked their brains
    To *find* ways to annoy us.
We want some job where pay is good
And we can work when in the mood ;
    But no !   They won't employ us.

[*Enter an Amateur Socialist.   He advances into the middle of the
stage and strikes an engaging attitude.*

THE AMATEUR SOCIALIST (*Recitative*).

        I see a crowd of men who look depressed a bit ;
            Shall I, then, let the chance that's offered go
        Of getting my opinions off my chest a bit ?
                No !
        Come, list to my address ;
        I bring you happiness.

45

Song.—An Amateur Socialist.

If you listen, I will tell you, as concisely as I can,
Of the numerous advantages accruing to my plan :
I'll free you from the evils which at present fairly pen you in ;
For I am a philanthropist. No other kinds are genuine.
I bring to every British home a flood of joy and sunniness,
A joyful lots-to-eat-ity and heaps-of-ready-money-ness.
Oh, a round of simple pleasure everybody's life will be
If only you have got sufficient sense to follow me.

Chorus of Unemployed (basso profundo).
Orl that we asks is liberty, so dear ;
Orl that we seeks is work—or else it's beer.

If you haven't got the money for to pay the weekly rent,
If the butcher or the grocer-man their small accounts have sent,
If the baker hints that cash is worth far more than pleasant promises,
If your little Billy's suit of clothes is wearing through (as Tommy's is),
If in one small room you're forced to live both stuffily and pokily,
If, in short, affairs are running—shall we put it ?—stoney brokily,
Then a thorough alteration in your fortunes you will see,
If only you have got sufficient sense to follow me.

Chorus of Unemployed.
It seems to us this cove's a real winner ;
Free drink he seems to mean, likewise free dinner.

The Unemployed. We're with you, guv'nor.
The Amateur Socialist. Stay, I forgot. All blessings I have
mentioned will fall upon you equally. There will be no distinctions
of rank, no private ownership, no bloated millionaires, but free meals,
free drinks——
A Workman. But how's it to be done ?
The Amateur Socialist. Quite simply. By work.
The Unemployed. Work ! ! !
The Amateur Socialist. All must labour, irrespective of rank.
There must be no idlers, no shirkers, no wastrels——
The Unemployed. 'Ere, let's bash the tyrant !
[*A wild rush is made at the Amateur Socialist, who flies, shrieking.*
Mr. Spender. A stupid fellow, letting them into the secret like that.
M. Bonhomme (*sadly*). Of course, work is necessary in any form of
government. But when speaking to the democracy the fact should be
concealed.
Mr. Spender. But is work necessary ?
M. Bonhomme. Not for the clevare men on the London County
Council, eh, Sir Spender ?

Mr. Spender (*after he has recovered from a hearty laugh*). Vous
êtes un joli chien.

M. Bonhomme. See! Ladies approach.

Mr. Spender. Peeresses, as I live! Proud and cruel dames,
descended from a line of robber barons—fair creatures, maybe, but
bloated by a self-consciousness of blue blood.

M. Bonhomme. A bas le blueblood!

[*Enter Lady Highflyer, née Miss Ermyntrude Pearl, of the
Frivolity Theatre, attended by Lady Scorcher, Lady Blazer,
and Lady Pauvreomme.*

Song : Lady Highflyer.

When I was a child, and went to school,
They always taught me this golden rule :
" A pretty face," they said, " is worth
An ocean of brains and a ton of birth ;
So watch your complexion carefullee,
And you'll be a leader of societee."

Chorus. So watch your complexion carefullee,
And you may be a ruler of societee.

I sang and danced for a year or so
As a humble member of the last back row ;
Till one of the principals left through pique,
And *I* got her part (one line) to speak.
I spoke that line so carefullee
That now I'm a leader of societee.

Chorus. She spoke that line in a manner free,
And now she's a ruler of societee.

I spoke that line till there came the days
Of the actresses' picture-postcard craze ;
I went to the leading firm, and they
Took photographs of me every day.
They photographed me so frequentlee
That now I'm a leader of societee.

Chorus. They photographed her so thoroughlee
That now she's a leader of societee.

You wouldn't believe how my postcards sold !
My fame was increased a thousandfold.
And the manager said, " Hullo, hullo !
She must play the lead in our next new show."
I played that lead so winsomelee
That now I'm a leader of societee.

Chorus. She played the lead so activelee
That now she's a leader of societee.

47

One night to supper I was taken by
The elderly Earl of Peckham Rye.
He simply lived in a front-row stall :
He bought me bouquets, and said, " Might he call ? "
I played that peer so artfullee
That now I'm a leader of societee.

Chorus. She played the knave so artfullee
That now she's a leader of societee.

M. BONHOMME. Clever girls ! My heart warms to them.

MR. SPENDER. But they are peeresses !

M. BONHOMME. From the *coulisses.* Tush, monsieur !

MR. SPENDER. And actresses ! !

M. BONHOMME. Well, what then ?

MR. SPENDER. The Nonconformist conscience——

M. BONHOMME. Mon Dieu, what are you, Sir Spender ? Reactionary, aristocrat, clerical—— ?

MR. SPENDER. Not at all, not at all, I assure you.

M. BONHOMME. Then you speak like one great big fool.

(*Curtain.*)

SCENE III.

The exterior of the Stock Exchange. Enter M. Bonhomme, wearing a worried look, accompanied by Mr. Spender.

M. BONHOMME (*wearily*). I trust, Sir Spender, that here we shall find a greater unanimity, a stronger support of your party, a wider love of the true spirit of humanitarianism and democracy.

MR. SPENDER (*earnestly*). Of course, of course.

M. BONHOMME. How rich is London ! Here are the prosperous men, those who think in millions. Ah, but who are these ? Millionaires, I doubt not.

MR. SPENDER. Not exactly, Mossoo. Yet they spend millions right nobly. They are the leading financiers——

M. BONHOMME. Of England, of the World ?

MR. SPENDER. No, of the London County Council. I rather fancy that they have come down here to raise a bit.

[*Enter Progressive members of the L.C.C., dancing gaily.*

Chorus : Progressive Members of the L.C.C.

We are subject like everyone else
To occasional fits of the blues ;
We know what it's like to awake with a shiver
At seven A.M. with a touch of the liver ;
Our studs, too, we frequently lose.
But all of these ills of the flesh
We are able at last to endure :
Things cannot go wrong with our spirits for long,
For we've found an infallible cure.

Raise a loan! Raise a loan!
    It's the only thing to do,
It's the finest mental pick-me-up that's known.
    If your tailor's bill's unpaid
    Don't be moody and dismayed:
Raise a loan! Raise a loan! Raise a loan!

M. BONHOMME. They seem, Sir Spender, to take their responsibilities lightly.

MR. SPENDER. And why not? It's not their money.

M. BONHOMME (*cautiously*). But it must be somebody's savings. Do the public love these spendthrifts?

MR. SPENDER. There *are* surly beggars, of course. Some folks are never satisfied, whatever you do for them.

M. BONHOMME. See these wild-eyed men who now approach. What are they? Bankrupts, I suppose.

MR. SPENDER. People who have investments and those sort of things. I haven't any myself. They don't get much sympathy from me.

[*Enter crowd in a state of great excitement.*

KAFFIR MARKET STOCKBROKERS.

A gentleman named Damocles,
    Of whom perhaps you've read,
Was noticeably ill at ease
    Because above his head,
When he was at the festive board,
There hung a dooced nasty sword.

Oh, Damocles! oh, Damocles!
    Your lot was better far:
Things never sank to twenty odd
    Which you had bought at par.

We hold a lot of Kaffir shares,
    And wish that we did not:
For, oh, it thins our whitening hairs,
    And makes us cold and hot
(Alternately) to see the way
The Government is making hay.

Oh, Damocles! oh, Damocles!
    You should have been content:
For *you* were never harried by
    A Liberal Government.

RAILWAY SHAREHOLDERS.
> And look on our distressful case,
> And see how sad we are
> For Socialism grows apace,
> And beats down every bar.
> And nobody would be surprised
> If railways soon were nationalised.

> Oh, Damocles ! Oh, Damocles !
> You got on very well :
> *You* never held a lot of stuff
> That you could never sell.

INDIA SHAREHOLDERS.
> The Government that rules to-day
> Despises me and you ;
> But loves with all its heart the gay
> And frolicsome Babu.
> He's only got to agitate,
> And *we* get ruined while you wait.

> Oh, Damocles ! Oh, Damocles !
> Your life was one long bliss ;
> *You* were not made to jump about
> By Governments like this.

ALL.
> Oh, Damocles ! Oh, Damocles !
> You weren't in such a fix
> As were the wretched City men
> Who lived in 1906.

M. BONHOMME. As a careful man, Sir Spender, a man who has worked hard and saved money, I must say I sympathise with them. Your Government——

MR. SPENDER. What, you dare to insinuate that our Government can do wrong ? Sir, be careful.

M. BONHOMME (*with dignity*). If you had been taught the principles, so simple, of political economy you would understand (*in a sudden outburst*) that you are a silly fat pig-dog.

[*Enter a banker, at whose respectable appearance Mr. Spender calms himself.*

M. BONHOMME (*addressing banker*). Pardon, monsieur, but can you tell me what has been the practical result of this Radical Government ?

Song.—THE BANKER.

If I had a friend with some money to spend,
　And he wished me to choose an investment,
" My boy," I should say, "listen closely, I pray,
　To advice which is all for the best meant.
If to get a return for your money you yearn,
　And if you don't wish to be bitten,
I think it is best all your cash to invest
　In something that's outside Great Britain."

That's the only rule for safety nowadays.
There's not another policy that pays.
　The golden rule, I'm sure it is,
　Runs ",Shun home in-securities."
It's the only rule for safety nowadays.

There was a glad time, in our glorious prime,
　When English investments were steady,
When our army and fleet were not easy to beat,
　And our motto was " Ready, aye ready."
But the Government now says, " It don't matter how
　Reduced is our Navy's condition ;
For it costs, does it not, such a terrible lot
　To put a new ship in commission."

So the only rule for safety nowadays,
The one and only policy that pays,
　Is " Remember every other land
　Is safer than the motherland."
That's the only rule for safety nowadays.

M. BONHOMME. I thank you, monsieur. (*With dignity*) Sir Spender, kindly summon for me a motor-cab.
MR. SPENDER. Why, you've a lot to see yet ! You shouldn't be so hasty. I want to show you——
M. BONHOMME. All I hope to see is Charing Cross.
MR. SPENDER. ? ?
M. BONHOMME. I desire to return to Paris. It seems to me the safer
B. FLETCHER ROBINSON.
P. G. WODEHOUSE.

Sources & Footnotes

[1] *A Fiscal Pantomime - The Sleeping Beauty*: *Daily Express*, 25 December 1903 (p. 4), published by Cyril Arthur Pearson (London). This playlet is a skit on the confused political situation brought about by Joseph Chamberlain and other supporters of the Tariff Reform League (TRL). A one-time prominent Liberal MP, Chamberlain had split the Party by resigning from Gladstone's administration in 1886 and taking with him a group known a Liberal Unionists (who supported his aim of rejecting Home Rule for Ireland). They began to work with the Conservative Party and Chamberlain was an effective and powerful member of the Conservative administration till he split the party in 1903 with his move to strengthen the Empire by imposing trade tariffs on countries outside the Empire ('Imperial Preference'). The point of this playlet is that both the TRL and their opponents, the Free Traders, wish to enlist the support of the Duke of Devonshire, a powerful political figure.

The first edition of the *Daily Express* newspaper was published on 24 April 1900. This 'New Morning London Newspaper' was founded by Pearson in response to a public demand for more information about events relating to the Second Boer War (1899-1902). Between 10 December 1899 and 15 December 1899, Boer Republicans inflicted a series of three defeats upon the British Army. Pearson reacted to news of 'Black Week' by dispatching seven War Correspondents to South Africa and these included 29 year-old Bertram Fletcher Robinson. During his four month deployment, Robinson sent thirteen dispatches to the *Daily Express* from Capetown and Graaf-Reinert. Upon his return to England, Robinson was promoted to 'Debut Editor' and given his own columns on page 4 of the 'London News' section. Between 4 May

1900 and 28 June 1904, Robinson bylined over one hundred items in the *Daily Express*.

[2] *Our Christmas Pantomime – Little Red Riding Hood; or, The Virtuous British Public and The Smart Set Wolf, Vanity Fair: A Weekly Show of Political, Social, and Literary Wares*, 8 December 1904 (pp. 731-734), published by Alfred Harmsworth (London). This playlet satirises the breakdown of Victorian values during the reign of King Edward VII. Many factors were involved. These included the increasing freedom for women (the Suffragette movement was growing ever stronger), new and sometimes shocking plays being shown in the theatre (Bernard Shaw, Ibsen, etc.), the growing habit of weekend house-parties where, it was widely believed, all sort of 'goings-on' went on; the freedom of movement brought by the motor car and the 'shocking' marriages between musical comedy stars/chorus girls and the aristocracy. All these elements were deeply disturbing to the respectable middle and lower-middle classes.

'*Vanity Fair*' was a weekly periodical that ran between 7 November 1868 and 5 February 1914. It was founded by Thomas Gibson Bowles and provided its readership with articles about fashion, current affairs, the theatre, books, social events and general trivia. 'Tommy' Bowles also used *Vanity Fair* to expose what he perceived to be the vanities of the elite social classes. Originally, his lampooning was confined to leading articles about the latest society scandal. However, from 30 January 1869, the magazine also featured caricatures of notable individuals together with satirical footnotes. These comments were bylined 'Jehu Junior', after a Biblical King who vanquished his enemies with extreme vigour. Ironically, many individuals felt flattered by their Jehu Junior. This was probably because the satire was humorous rather than malicious. Between 26 May 1904 and 24 October 1906, Bertram Fletcher Robinson edited one hundred and twenty-six issues of *'Vanity Fair'* and bylined sixty-eight items that appeared therein.

[3] *A Winter's Tale – King Arthur & His Court: Vanity Fair: A Weekly Show of Political, Social, and Literary Wares*, 14 December 1905 (pp. 778-781), published by Alfred Harmsworth (London). This playlet is a satire on the large number of political groups that opposed Arthur Balfour during late 1905. Balfour, a nephew of the Marquess of Salisbury, was an experienced politician who became Prime Minister (Conservative) when Salisbury resigned on 11 July 1902. He inherited the problem of Home Rule for Ireland which had drawn off members of the Liberal Party into a new group known as the Liberal Unionists. The Liberal Unionists joined the Conservatives on many issues (the Unionist alliance) and even formed part of the Conservative Cabinet before the Liberal Unionist, Joseph Chamberlain, split his Party with his support for the TRL and Imperial Preference. Balfour's Cabinet lost so many members that he resigned on 5 December 1905 and Henry Campbell-Bannerman formed a new Liberal Government. By the time this playlet was published, the new administration had been in power for nine days. It won a landslide victory in the General Election of January 1906, mainly on the basis that so many factions wanted the Conservatives out.

It is probable that it required two or three days to print each weekly edition of *Vanity Fair*. The conclusion to *A Winter's Tale* leaves the reader in doubt as to whether Balfour or Campbell-Bannermann was victorious in their battle. Hence it appears that Fletcher Robinson and Wodehouse wrote this piece shortly *before* Balfour resigned and Campbell-Bannerman was appointed Prime Minister (5 December 1905). But, although it was already out of date before publication, perhaps Fletcher Robinson exercised his editorial prerogative and went ahead anyway?

[4] *The Progressive's Progress – Some Memories of 1906*: *The World – A Journal for Men and Women*, 1 January 1907 (pp. 8-11), published by Alfred Harmsworth (London). This playlet satirises two topics that excited Londoners during 1906. The first of these was the *Entente Cordiale*, a historic alliance that was agreed between the United Kingdom and France during 1904. The second topic was the growing increase in expenditure by the London County Council (LCC) that was beginning to alarm Londoners.

The LCC was founded in 1889 and re-organised during 1900. The majority of seats were held by the Progressive Party, the name adopted by an alliance of Liberals and Radical groups that focused upon municipal rather than national issues. The LCC rapidly expanded its control over transport, schools and rebuilding projects, all of which were needed but entailed significant expenditure. By creating their own labour force to oversee this work, the LCC became London's biggest employer. While the aim was praiseworthy, local ratepayers felt matters were proceeding too fast and at too much cost. Just before *The Progressive's Progress* was published, it became known that the LCC had bought a large area of land on the south side of Westminster Bridge and was planning to build a County Hall as big as the Houses of Parliament across the river. For many Londoners, this was too much. Within months of this playlets's publication, the Progressive Party lost their majority on the LCC and they never regained it.

'*The World*' was a weekly periodical that ran between 1874 and 1922. It was founded by E. H. Yates and E. C. Grenville Murray but the former soon became the sole editor and proprietor. *The World* published society news and gossip. However, following its acquisition by Alfred Harmsworth (Lord Northcliffe), the paper also featured both literary items and news. During late October 1906, Bertram Fletcher Robinson became editor of '*The World*' and his position at *Vanity Fair* passed to Frank Harris.

Source Acknowledgements

All four playlets are republished from items that were collected by this book's compiler. *A Fiscal Pantomime: The Sleeping Beauty*, is a facsimile of a microfiche image that has since been electronically enhanced to make it as legible as possible. This approach was adopted because it was feared that any attempt at transcription might have led to the introduction of typographical errors.

The remaining three playlets are also facsimiles of the original texts. However, all four playlets were originally published in large tabloid format, so it was necessary to resize them. This work, and the digital enhancement of *A Fiscal Pantomime: The Sleeping Beauty* was diligently undertaken by Bob Gibson at staunchdesign: 11 Shipton Road, Woodstock, Oxford, Oxfordshire, OX20 1LW.

All four playlets are republished in strict accordance with the terms and conditions that have been imposed under a ten-year license that was kindly granted to this book's compiler by the theatrical representatives of the Estate of PG Woodhouse as follows:

Textual Annotations

The index number before each annotation comprises of two parts. The first part indicates the page upon which the annotated item can be located. The second part, after the decimal point, indicates the line number on that page upon which the item commences. Headings are included within the line count. Quotation marks and ellipses have been omitted from the referenced quotations.

1.8 ~ The Free Fooders. A term used to describe opponents of Tariff-Reform and Imperial Preference. Free Fooders argued that hefty duties on imported goods would mean dearer food, especially bread ('Corn Tax').

1.10 ~ Cobden Club. A political gentlemen's club in London. It was founded in 1866 for believers in the Free Trade doctrine. The club was named in honour of Richard Cobden (1804-1865), a British manufacturer, Radical and Liberal statesman (see Figure 1). Because of its Free Trade connection, the Cobden Club mainly attracted Liberals as members, but with the fading of both the Liberals as a national force, and of Free Trade as a popular cause, the club fell into decline during the twentieth century. Like many other gentlemen's clubs, it went through substantial financial difficulties during the late 1970s, and closed at the end of that decade.

1.14 ~ we should do by the Yank & German as they now do to us; Both the United States of America and Germany operated strict tariff protections and access to their markets, but each was vociferously opposed to the introduction of a reciprocal system within the British Empire. In essence, the USA and Germany operated single trading blocs.

Figure 1. Richard Cobden (c. 1855).

1.18 ~ Chamberlain. Joseph Chamberlain (1836-1914). His staunch support for Imperial Preference and Tariff-Reform led to the split of the Liberal Unionist Party in 1903 and also the collapse of the Conservative-led government in 1905 (see Figure 2).

1.22 ~ the Cobden Press. This was the publishing arm of the Cobden Club. Under the co-editorship of John Bright (1811-1889), one of the club's early patrons, the Cobden Press published Cobden's collected speeches during 1870.

1.23 ~ Free Food League. A Unionist pressure group (Liberal Unionists and Conservatives) that was founded in 1903 to oppose the Tarrif-Reform League. Influential members included the Conservative MP, Lord Hugh Cecil. He was a son of Lord Salisbury, the Conservative Prime Minister whose final term in that office ended on 11 July 1902.

Figure 2. The Rt. Hon. Joseph Chamberlain (c. 1890).

Figure 3. Spencer Compton Cavendish,
8th Duke of Devonshire (c. 1890).

1.24 ~ Ch-tsw-rth. Chatsworth House is a large country house at Chatsworth, Derbyshire, England. It is the seat of the Dukes of Devonshire, and has been home to their family, the Cavendish family, since 1549 when Bess of Hardwick settled at Chatsworth.

1.25 ~ the Duke of D-v-nsh-r-. Spencer Cavendish (1833-1908), 8th Duke of Devonshire and the leader of the Liberal Party till 1886 (see Figure 3). That same year, he split from the Liberals over the question of Irish Home Rule and then led the splinter Liberal Unionist Party till 1903. A man of massive political influence, Devonshire declined the premiership three times. Between 1902 and 1903, he also led the Unionists in the House of Lords and accepted a Cabinet position within Lord Salisbury's Conservative Cabinet. He resigned his Cabinet post on 1 October 1903 but did not openly oppose Chamberlain and Tariff-Reform till March 1904. This is why, in December 1903, he is depicted as being wooed by both Liberals and Conservatives.

1.29 ~ Sir Michael Hicks Beach. Michael Hicks Beach (1837-1916), was a former Conservative Chancellor of the Exchequer (1895-1902). He was unpopular because he levied taxes on sugar, corn and flour in order to finance British military operations during the Second Boer War (1899-1902). Beach left government upon the retirement of Lord Salisbury in July 1902 (see Figure 4).

1.30 ~ Sir Henry Campbell-Bannerman. Henry Campbell-Bannerman (1836-1908) was the leader of the Liberal Party (1899-1908) and a staunch Free Trader. He hoped that Devonshire's dislike of Chamberlain's Tariff-Reform policy would persuade him to return to the main Liberal Party (see Figure 5).

1.31 ~ the Tariff Reform League. The TRL was a pressure group formed in 1903 to protest against 'unfair' foreign imports. It campaigned for taxation on foreign goods to protect British industry from foreign competition (Imperial Preference). The TRL was well funded and included politicians, intellectuals and businessmen. It was popular with the grassroots of the Conservative Party and numbered 250,000 members by 1914. Chamberlain was the most vocal proponent of the TRL and Cyril Pearson (Fletcher Robinson's employer) was its first Chairman.

Figure 4. Michael Beach, 1st Earl St. Aldwyn (1885).

2.5 ~ The "Standard". This was a national daily newspaper that was printed in London and first published on 21 May 1827. The first proprieter of the paper was Charles Baldwin. However, it was under the subsequent ownership of James Johnstone that *The Standard* became a morning paper (29 June 1857). On 11 June 1859, Baldwin also published the first edition of the *Evening Standard*. In 1904, Cyril Pearson purchased both *The*

Standard and *Evening Standard* for £700,000. Pearson then merged the *Evening Standard* with his *St James Gazette* and he altered the Conservative bias of both newspapers to a pro-Liberal one.

SIR HENRY CAMPBELL-BANNERMAN. 1899.

Figure 5. Henry Campbell Bannermann as drawn by Leslie Ward ('Spy') for '*Vanity Fair*' (1899).

2.9 ~ Lord Ros-b-ry. Archibald Philip Primrose (1847-1929), 5th Earl of Rosebery. He was a prominent Liberal MP and succeeded William Gladstone as Prime Minister during March 1894. However, he resigned in June 1895, almost certainly because he lost Liberal support when he tried to expand the Royal Navy. Rosebery then turned to writing as the *Ploughman's Song* states (see Figure 6).

Figure 6. Lord Rosebery. Drawn by
Leslie Ward for 'Vanity Fair' (1901).

2.10 ~ The Parrot. Between early October and mid
December 1903, the *Daily Express* published more than
forty poems under the heading of 'The Parrot'. These
verses always appeared on the front page and frequently
referred to the debate between Tariff-Reformists and Free
Fooders ('Fiscal Policy'). They also featured a
'wonderful parrot' that repeatedly exclaimed 'Your Food
will cost you more'. Records reveal that Wodehouse
penned nineteen of these poems and it seems likely that
Fletcher Robinson also contributed to the series. The
Parrot poems became a national craze and the *Daily
Express* offered a prize of £25 to anyone who taught a
parrot to repeat the slogan, 'Your Food will cost you
more'.

2.12 ~ Herr Spoofheimer. A likely reference to George Goschen, 1st Viscount Goschen (1831-1907). He was a Liberal MP (1863–1886) but resigned from Gladstone's Cabinet over the question of Home Rule for Ireland. In 1887, Goschen became a Liberal Unionist MP and he served in the Conservative Government till it fell in 1892. Unable to work alongside Chamberlain, Goschen joined the Conservative Party during 1893. Although he retired in 1900, Goschen continued to publicly criticise both Chamberlain and the Tariff-Reform movement (see Figure 7).

PUNCH'S FANCY PORTRAITS.–No. 44.

RIGHT HON. G. JOACHIM GOSCHEN, M.P.

This is a Joke-'im Goschen Picture of a Wise Man from the East, at present ascertaining which way the Wind blows.

Figure 7. George Joachim Goschen,
1st Viscount Goschen as depicted in *Punch* (1881).

2.14 ~ the Pavilion of the Sleeping Beauty. Totally round marquees, called pavilions, dotted the landscape during the glory days of English longbowmen. They can be seen in dozens of oil paintings dating back to the 13th Century. Often profusely decorated with woven, striped cloth, embroidery and applied motifs, the pavilions created a colourful scene. Such tents were sometimes pitched in Chatsworth Park near a summer house called Queen Mary's Bower. This structure was a favourite place of Mary Queen of Scots when she was imprisoned by the Earl of Shrewsbury at Chatsworth House (1570-1584).

2.30 ~ Lord George? Lord George Hamilton (1845-1927) held the position of Secretary of State for India under Arthur Balfour. However, he resigned this post during 1903 in protest over Balfour's refusal to commit himself to either Free Trade or Tariff-Reform. Thereafter, Hamilton held the honorary post of Major of Deal (1909), received honorary degrees from both Glasgow and Oxford University and was appointed a Justice of the Peace.

2.33 ~ Lord George Sanger. George Sanger (1825-1911) was a well-known circus impresario. During 1898, he became embroiled in a lawsuit with William Frederick Cody ('Buffalo Bill'). Sanger was infuriated that Cody's counsel referred to his client as 'The Honourable Colonel Cody'. In response, Sanger announced that he would call himself Lord George Sanger in future and he did so. Everybody thought that Queen Victoria would be furious at a showman adopting the style of address of a younger son of a duke but, apparently, she was highly amused. Sanger's Circus persisted till 1962.

2.36 ~ the Hippodrome. This London theatre stood at the corner of Charing Cross Road and Leicester Square. It was opened in 1900 and it specialised in variety and animal acts that included elephants and polar bears. The building was converted into a nightclub and restaurant complex during 1983.

3.14 ~ THE PLOUGHMAN: I will sing it to you. This is an allusion to a line that precedes the song, "A Magnet Hung in a Hardware Shop" from *Patience* by Gilbert and Sullivan:

> **ANGELA** (wildly): But we don't know the fable of the Magnet and the Churn!
> **GROSVENOR**: Don't you? Then I will sing it to you.'

Patience was the sixth of fourteen operatic collaborations between Gilbert and Sullivan (1871-1896). It opened at the Opera Comique in London on 23 April 1881 before relocating to the 1,292-seat Savoy Theatre in the Strand (near Fleet Street and the former offices of the *Daily Express*). *Patience* was the first theatrical production in the world to be lit entirely by electric light.

3.15 ~ THE PLOUGHMAN'S SONG. This song is a close parody of "A Wandering Minstrel I" from *The Mikado*. This was the ninth of fourteen comic operas by Gilbert and Sullivan. *The Mikado* opened on 14 March 1885 at the Savoy Theatre and ran for 672 performances.

3.26 ~ Oh, willow, willow. This is an allusion to the line 'Oh, sorrow, sorrow!' in "A Wandering Minstrel I" from *The Mikado*. It also alludes to the line 'Willow, titwillow, titwillow!' in Ko-Ko's song, "On a Tree by a River" from that same opera.

3.32 ~ My celebrated sneer's surpassed by few. This line is an allusion to the phrase 'celebrated sneer' from the song, "If you give me your attention" in *'Princess Ida'*. This was the eighth of fourteen comic operas by Gilbert and Sullivan. It opened on 5 January 1884 at the Savoy Theatre and ran for 246 performances. *Princess Ida* is the only three act Gilbert and Sullivan opera and the only one with dialogue in blank verse.

3.34 ~ But if strenuous activity is needed. This is an allusion to the line 'But if patriotic sentiment is needed' in "A Wandering Minstrel I" from *The Mikado*.

4.19 ~ There are more things in heaven and earth, Horatio, than are dreamt of in your philosophy. A direct quote from Act I (Scene V) in *Hamlet* (c. 1600). This was Shakespeare's longest play and it explores the themes of treachery, revenge, incest, and moral corruption.

5.12 ~ my jaegers. Dr. Gustave Jaeger (1832-1917) was a German Professor of Zoology and Physiology at the University of Stuttgart. He advocated wearing wool next to the skin, for warmth and also to absorb perspiration. Jaeger believed that wearing silk, cotton or linen would cause the wearer to perspire more and then reabsorb the unpleasant bodily vapours back into their body. Oscar Wilde and George Bernard Shaw spoke in favour of the idea and men started wearing what we now call 'Long Johns', a single body-length article of underwear.

5.13 ~ Aroint the wretch!. A parody upon the line 'Aroint thee, witch' from Act I (Scene III) of Macbeth (c. 1605). This was Shakespeare's shortest play and it deals with the themes of bravery, ambition, murder, arrogance, guilt, madness, death and retribution.

5.33 ~ Volapuk. An international language that was devised by a German Roman Catholic Priest called Father Johann Martin Schleyer (1879-1880). It had some success but was soon overtaken by Esperanto.

5.39 ~ John Bull's Store. This is a reference to "The John Bull Store Song" by Bertram Fletcher Robinson (see Appendix A). The fictional character of John Bull (or 'Johnny' Bull) was held by many to be the personification of the patriotic Englishman (see Figure 8). He was conceived in 1712 by a London-based physician called John Arbuthnot (1667-1735) and also features within the works of the American cartoonist Thomas Nast (1840-1902) and the Irish writer George Bernard Shaw (1856-1950). The music for "The John Bull Store Song" was composed by Robert Eden and the score was arranged by George Byng. It was published by Elkin & Company Limited of London and most of the proceeds were donated to the TRL.

Figure 8. This political engraving by William Charles depicts 'Johnny' Bull as an American plunderer (1814).

6.1 ~ SONG OF THE COBDEN CLUB. The metre and much of the rhyming scheme for this song is derived from "God Save the Queen" (or "God Save the King" as it was when the playlet was written). It is the UK national anthem and also that of her territories, dependencies and some Commonwealth realms. The first definitive published version of the present tune appeared in 1744 in *Thesaurus Musicus*.

8.2 ~ Well, we're here now, and there she lies. The first speech of Act II continues in the same metre as "The Song of the Cobden Club" that draws Act I to a close.

9.42 ~ Chamberlain is THE leader of the Unionst party! The Duke of Devonshire was the formal leader of the Liberal Unionist Party. This Liberal faction had split from the main Liberal Party over the question of Home Rule for Ireland. The Liberal Unionists formed a coalition with the Conservative Party during Balfour's premiership (1902-1905) and they urged reform in Home affairs. Devonshire was concerned by Chamberlain's growing popularity amongst Liberal Unionists, and he eventually resigned from the leadership of the group in early 1904.

10.16 ~ bold as radium. Radium is a radioactive element that was discovered by Marie Skłodowska-Curie and her husband Pierre in 1898. The discovery of radium led to intense excitement throughout the scientific community. In 1903, Marie Curie received the Nobel Prize in Physics and she later won the Nobel Prize in Chemistry (1911). Marie Curie remains one of only three double Nobel Prize Laureates.

10.32 ~ We are a happy Free Food League! We are! We are! We are! In January 1906, Wodehouse had a poem published that is entitled *The Phalanx*. It is a satirical comment upon the deeply divided Conservative

Cabinet of late 1905. Each verse ends: 'We are a happy Cabinet! We are! We are!! We are!!!'.

12.8 ~ GRANDMOTHER: Mrs. Grundy. This is a reference to the 'unseen character' of that same name in a play entitled *Speed the Plough* (1798) by Thomas Morton (1764-1838). Mrs. Grundy is the personification of both respectability and propriety.

12.9 ~ GOOD FAIRY: Mr. W. T. Stead. William Thomas Stead (1849-1912) was a British Reformist, journalist, spiritualist and the founder of the *Review of Reviews* (1890). He was well acquainted with Fletcher Robinson's friend, Sir Arthur Conan Doyle and reportedly acted as both his 'collaborator and combatant'. Stead died aboard the *RMS Titanic* on 15 March 1912 (see Figure 9).

12.10 ~ DEMONS: Messers. Pinero, Maeterlinck, Jones, Ibsen. All three men are now the acclaimed authors of what some Victorians perceived to be new and 'disturbing' social plays: Arthur Wing Pinero (1855-1934), Maurice Maeterlinck (1862-1949), Henry Arthur Jones (1851-1929) and Henrik Ibsen (1828-1906). [see Figures 10-13].

Figure 9. William Thomas
Stead (c. 1910).

Figure 10. Arthur Wing
Pinero (1892).

Figure 11. Maurice
Maeterlinck (c. 1930).

Figure 12. Henry Arthur   Figure 13. Henrik
Jones (c. 1880).   Ibsen (c. 1890).

12.11 ~ HUNTERS: Messers. Benson, R. J. Campbell, Sutro. All three men were the authors of popular and 'moral' Victorian plays. Edward Frederick Benson (1867-1940) was a prolific author; his 'Mapp and Lucia' stories are still popular (see Figure 14). Reginald John Campbell (1867-1936) was a well known Congregational clergyman (see Figure 15). Alfred Sutro (1863-1933) wrote cynical plays that satirised 'High Society' (see Figure 16).

12.12 ~ Mesdames Corelli and Rita. Marie Corelli (1855-1924) was a best-selling author of many novels in which, good always prevailed over evil (see Figure 17). 'Rita' was the pseudonym of the writer Eliza Margaret J. Humphreys née Gollan (1850-1938). She was a prolific writer of light fiction.

Figure 14. Edward F. Benson (c. 1895).

Figure 15. R. J. Campbell by Leslie Ward (1904).

Figure 16. Alfred Sutro (c. 1915).

Figure 17. Marie Corelli (1906).

12.14 ~ WOLF: The Smart Set. A group of people that included members of the aristocracy and the 'New Money' men; manufacturers and financiers whom previously Society had ignored but whose vast wealth meant they could no longer be overlooked. Many had been members of the raffish 'Marlborough House Set', the group that clustered round King Edward VII (1841-1910) when he was Prince of Wales (see Figure 18).

Figure 18. Albert Edward, Prince of Wales (c. 1900).

12.22 ~ To us, my friends, your kind attention lend. An allusion to "The Prologue" in W. S. Gilbert's play entitled *The Wicked World* (1873) which begins: 'The Author begs you'll kind attention pay/While I explain the object of his play.'

13.15 ~ SONG. LITTLE RED RIDING HOOD. This song contains allusions to Gilbert and Sullivan. For example the line 'I've heard of the ways of that wonderful coterie' uses the same metre and rhyme scheme as 'If you want a receipt for that popular mystery' from "The Heavy Dragoon" song in *Patience* (1881).

13.46 ~ a Yarborough. This is hand at Bridge where the highest card held is a nine. In September 1901, *Pearson's Magazine* published an article entitled 'On Card Games and Others' that was written by Fletcher Robinson.

16.31 ~ Don't talk of your Barries or Your Marshalls and Hoods. All three men wrote popular plays that were 'suitable for all the family': James Matthew Barrie (1860-1937), Francis Albert Marshall (1840-1899) and Basil Hood (1864-1917).

17.37 ~ Who love to read about the Upper Ten. During 1875, Kelly & Co. of London published the first edition of an annual social register, *The Upper Ten Thousand.* From 1878, all new editions were renamed *Kelly's Handbook to the Titled, Landed & Official Classes.* Nevertheless, the term 'Upper Ten' persisted and it was widely used to refer to people 'in Society'.

19.1 ~ If you dance to the tune of Sir Francis Jeune. Sir Francis Jeune (1843-1905), 1st Baron St. Helier was President of the Divorce Court (1892-1905).

21.26 ~ I notice you are reading "Gyp,". The nom de plume of the well known French writer, Sibylle-Gabrielle Marie-Antoinette de Riqueti de Mirabeau, Comtesse de Martel de Janville (1849-1932).

21.39 ~ *Mutantur tempora, nos et Mutamur* (change) *in illis.* This is an allusion to the Latin adage 'Tempora mutantur et nos mutamur in illis', which translates to: Times change and we change with them. The expression was rewritten to fit the English rhyme scheme. Fletcher Robinson and Wodehouse both studied Latin prose during their schooling.

23.2 ~ You've seen "The Walls of Jericho,". This is a reference to Alfred Sutro's most popular play (1904).

26.5 ~ King Arthur. Arthur James Balfour (1848-1930), 1st Earl of Balfour was a Conservative MP and statesman (see Figure 19). He authored the tough Perpetual Crimes Act (1887) that aimed to prevent boycotts, intimidation or unlawful assembly in Ireland during the Irish Land War (1879-1882). On 11 July 1902, Balfour became Prime Minister following the resignation of Lord Salisbury from that office. His premiership was marred by deep divisions within the Cabinet over the issue of Tariff-Reform. Balfour resigned during December 1905 and he was succeeded by Sir Henry Campbell-Bannerman.

Figure 19. Arthur James Balfour (c. 1905).

26.8 ~ Merlin (*out of a job*). This is a reference to Spencer Cavendish, 8th Duke of Devonshire, who retired from Balfour's Cabinet during 1903 (see **1.25**).

26.9 ~ Sir Kaye. Charles Vane-Tempest-Stewart (1852-1915), 6th Marquess of Londonderry (see Figure 20) was a Conservative MP. He was Lord President of the Council (1903-1905) during Balfour's premiership (1902-1905). Londonderry was an outspoken critic of both Irish Home Rule and John Redmond, the leader of the Irish Parliamentary Party.

Figure 19. The 6th Marquess of Londonderry (1902)

26.12 ~ Sir Campbell (*a noted Scot*). Henry Campbell-Bannerman (see **1.30**) was the Liberal Prime Minister. In January 1906, he won a landslide victory against his Conservative predecessor, Arthur Balfour. During that election, Balfour lost his seat and only 157 Conservatives were returned to the House of Commons (two-thirds of these supported Joseph Chamberlain and Tariff-Reform).

26.13 ~ Sir Primrose (*acultivated Pict*). Archibald Philip Primrose, 5th Earl of Rosebery. He succeeded Gladstone as Liberal Prime Minister in 1894 but was unhappy in that role. Rosebery resigned the premiership during 1895 and then became a writer (see **2.9**).

26.14 ~ Sir Lloyd (*a Cymric*). David Lloyd George (1863-1945), 1st Earl Lloyd-George of Dwyfor (see Figure 21) was a Liberal MP and the only ever Welsh Prime Minister of the United Kingdom (1916-1922). He gained national fame because of his vehement opposition to the Second Boer War (1899-1902). George also accused Joseph Chamberlain, the then Secretary of State for the Colonies, of 'war profiteering'. The Chamberlain family-run company (Kynochs Ltd.) had won tenders to the War Office though its prices were higher than some of its competitors. Following a speech given to a meeting in Chamberlain's constituency, George had to be disguised as a policeman in order to conceal him from an angry mob.

26.15 ~ Sir Redmond (*The Irish Chief*). John Edmond Redmond (1856-1914), was a British MP (see Figure 22). He led the Irish Parliamentary Party (1900-1918) and campaigned for a Dublin-based Irish Parliament to take care of domestic affairs. However, Redmond also wanted to maintain links with Britain in order to retain Free Trade. During 1914, he secured the Third Irish Home Rule Bill that granted an interim form of self-government to Ireland. However, the implementation of Irish Home Rule was delayed until 1921 by the intervention of World War I (1914-1918) and the Easter Rising in Dublin (1916).

26.16 ~ Sir Grey (*a patriotic Goth*). Edward Grey (1862-1933), 1st Viscount Grey of Fallodon was a Liberal MP. In December 1905, he was appointed Secretary of State for Foreign Affairs by Henry Campell-Bannerman and he held that office for eleven years. When Campbell-

Bannerman resigned the premiership in 1908, Grey was tipped to succeed him. However, that post was eventually awarded to Herbert Asquith (1852-1928).

Figure 21. David Lloyd George (1919).   Figure 22. John Edmond Redmond (1906).

26.17 ~ Sir Keir (*an advanced Hun*). James Keir Hardie (1856-1915) was a Scottish Independent Socialist (see Figure 23). During 1900, he helped to found the Labour Representation Committee and became the first Labour MP. The Liberal leader, Henry Campbell-Bannerman was concerned that this new party might split the anti-Conservative vote. Hence, he agreed a 'Lib-Lab pact' and declined to stand against Labour in thirty constituencies in the 1906 election (a landslide victory to the Liberal Party).

26.18 ~ Sir Winston (*a conspirator*). Sir Winston Leonard Spencer-Churchill (1874-1965) was a soldier and war correspondent before becoming a Conservative MP in 1900 (see Figure 24). During his first parliamentary session, Churchill opposed Joseph Chamberlain over Tariff-Reform. In 1904, he crossed the floor to sit as a member of the Liberal Party and continue campaigning for Free Trade. When Campbell-Bannerman took office in 1905, Churchill was appointed Under-Secretary of State for the Colonies. He rejoined the Conservatives in 1925 and was Prime Minister twice (1940-1945 & 1951-1955).

Figure 23. Keir Hardie (c. 1914).   Figure 24. Winston Churchill (1904).

27.44 ~ A host with but a single aim/We fight in perfect unity. This is an allusion to the following lines in the song "Of Happiness the Very Pith" from *The Gondoliers* by Gilbert and Sullivan:

Marco & Giuseppe.
Two kings, of undue pride bereft,
Who act in perfect unity.'

The Gondoliers was the twelfth of fourteen comic operatic collaborations between Gilbert and Sullivan. It premiered at the Savoy Theatre on 7 December 1889 and ran for a very successful 554 performances. *The Gondoliers* is widely considered to be Gilbert and Sullivan's last great success.

28.9 ~ Our loyalty's free from defect,/Our morals are highly correct. This is an allusion to the following lines in the song "Miya Sama, Miya Sama" from *The Mikado* by Gilbert and Sullivan (see **3.15**):

Mikado
My morals have been declared
Particularly correct;

and

Mikado
My nature is love and light —
My freedom from all defect —

36.1 ~ SONG: KING ARTHUR. This song is a comment upon the major reorganisation that was taking place within the British Army about the time it was written. These changes were being implemented in response to concerns over Imperial policing rather than military strategy. For example, the British Government was worried about the Ottoman Empire, whose territory bordered the Suez Canal, a vital British-owned trade route.

36.2 ~ Oh, the life of a king is not skittles and beer at all. This line has a similar metre and rhyme scheme to 'If you want a receipt for that popular mystery' from "The Heavy Dragoon" song in *Patience* by Gilbert and Sullivan (see **3.14**).

36.17 ~ Feeling himself on the verge of insanity? An allusion to the following line from "The Sorcerer's Song" in *The Sorcerer* by Gilbert and Sullivan:

John Wellington Wells
Driving your foes to the verge of insanity.

The Sorcerer was the third of fourteen comic operatic collaborations between Gilbert and Sullivan. It opened on 17 November 1877 at the Opera Comique in the Strand in London, where it ran for 178 performances. For the 1884 revival, Gilbert and Sullivan abridged the ending to Act I and provided a new opening to Act II, and it is in this form that the work is usually presented today.

36.30 ~ Are the Chinese on the Rand flogged diurnally? In 1904, it was reported that ten thousand Chinese labourers had been brought to South Africa to provide cheap labour for the gold mines. It soon became clear that their working conditions were little short of slavery and there was a public outcry in both Britain and abroad when the news got out. During July 1904, Fletcher Robinson bylined an article entitled 'On Political Lies – A Growing Danger in British Politics' for *Vanity Fair*. In this piece he questions whether the data pertaining to the number of Chinese labourers working the mines had been exaggerated for political reasons.

36.31 ~ Straphanger. This was a colloquial term used to describe a commuter who was compelled to stand whilst travelling upon the overcrowded London public transport network.

36.32 ~ Do the "All Backs" play quite fair in the scrum? The first New Zealand 'All Blacks' rugby team to tour Britain during 1905, are still a legend. They played thirty-five games and only lost once to Wales. During January 1889, Bertram Fletcher Robinson watched a rugby match between Devon and the Maoris (the precursor to the 'All Blacks'). This game involved one of his teachers, Edward Norman Gardiner (1864-1930). The match was played at Exeter in-front of several thousand spectators and the Maoris won (0-13). Later, Fletcher Robinson wrote a book entitled *Rugby Football* (London:

A.D. Innes & Co. Ltd.) and recalled that during this match (p. 305):

> One of the Devon forwards came off the field sorrowfully rubbing his leg. "What is the matter?" I asked. "Why," he said, "I came to play football, not to join in a dog fight! One of the beggars has bitten me in the calf!"

36.46 ~ We ask/suggest,/insist,/demand that you. An allusion to the following dialogue from Act I of *The Gondoliers* by Gilbert and Sullivan (see **27.44**):

DUKE
And suite-have arrived at Venice, and seek-

CASILDA
Desire-

DUCHESS
Demand!

DUKE
And demand an audience.

38.4 ~ *Old Palace Yard, Westminster.* The Palace Yard, Westminster is also the setting for Act II of *Iolanthe* by Gilbert and Sullivan. It was their seventh of fourteen collaborations. *Iolanthe* opened at the Savoy Theatre, on 25 November 1882, three days after *Patience* closed, and it ran for 398 performances. It was the first Gilbert and Sullivan opera to be premiered at the Savoy Theatre.

38.5 ~ *M. Pierre Bonhomme.* This is a probable reference to Dr. Paul Brousse (1844-1912), the socialist President of the Paris Council and a member of the French Section of the Workers' International (see Figure 25).

Between 16 October 1905 and 21 October 1905, Monsieur Brousse led a large delegation of Parisian Councillors to London. During that visit, the French delegation toured various London County Council funded projects including schools and utility companies (see Appendix B).

Figure 25. Dr. Paul Brousse Figure 26. Will Crooks
(c. 1910). (c. 1900).

38.6 ~ *Mr. Will Spender M.P., L.C.C.* One of the disturbing features of the London County Council, so far as the middle-class ratepayers were concerned, was the large number of Socialist trade unionists in positions of authority. Based purely on the coincidence of the first name, the authors might have based the character of Will Spender upon one Will Crooks (1852-1921). He was a staunch Trade Unionist, first Labour Mayor of Poplar, an MP and a long-time member of the LCC (see Figure 26). Alternatively, Will Spender might have been based upon Sir Edwin Andrew Cornwall (1863-1953). He was elected to the Chairmanship of the LCC in 1904 (Progressive Party) and became a Liberal MP in 1906 (see Figure 27).

38.16 ~ But tell me, Monsieur, is it true that which we hear...that your country, so beautiful, rejoices in her

bold fraternal Government...that all are satisfied in England? This is an allusion to the following dialogue in *Utopia, Limited* by Gilbert and Sullivan:

CALYNX

Good news! Great news! His Majesty's eldest daughter, Princess Zara, who left our shores five years since to go to England the greatest, the most powerful, the wisest country in the world...

Utopia, Limited was the thirteenth of fourteen comic operas by Gilbert and Sullivan. It premiered on 7 October 1893 at the Savoy Theatre and ran for 245 performances. This work did not achieve the same level of success as many of the previous Gilbert and Sullivan productions but it still yielded a profit.

Figure 27. Sir Edwin Andrew Cornwall (1919).　Figure 28. John Burns (c. 1911).

39.8 ~ John Burns. John Burns (1858-1943) was a British trade unionist politician and historian (see Figure 28). Together with Will Crooks (1852-1921) and Ben Tillett (1860-1943), he played a leading part in The Great

Docks Strike of 1889 and was regarded by many as a rabble-rousing firebrand. In fact, all three men were practical politicians who they worked well with the Liberals on the LCC and did much good work.

39.20 ~ When I was but a lad, I told my father. This parodies the Gilbert and Sullivan song, "When a Felon's not Engaged in his Employment" from *The Pirates of Penzance*. This was the fifth of fourteen collaborations between Gilbert and Sullivan. It was officially premiered at the Fifth Avenue Theatre in New York on 31 December 1879 and was an instant hit with both audiences and critics alike. The London premiere was held on 3 April 1880, at the Opera Comique, where it ran for 363 performances. In 1981, *The Pirates of Penzance* was revived for Broadway by the American theatrical producer and director, Joseph Papp (1921-1991). This show ran for 787 performances and it won the Tony Award for Best Revival.

39.26 ~ How true is that remark of Mr. Gilbert. Between 1871 and 1896, William Schwenck Gilbert (1836–1911) and Arthur Seymour Sullivan (1842–1900) wrote fourteen comic operas. Gilbert (1836–1911) was the librettist (see Figure 29) and Sullivan (see Figure 30) was the composer. The four Bobbles & Playlets include allusions to all but one of the Gilbert and Sullivan operas that were written between 1877 and 1893 (the omitted item is the 1888 production, *The Yeomen of the Guard*). There is also an allusion to 'The Prologue' from Gilbert's play, *The Wicked World* (see **12.22**). It is probable that Wodehouse contributed these allusions because William Townend, his friend and roommate at Dulwich College (1894-1900), reported that Wodehouse was a Gilbert fan.

Figure 29. Sir W. S. Gilbert   Figure 30. Sir A. S.
(c. 1886).   Sullivan (c. 1895).

39.29 ~ With women I am diffident and shy. This is an allusion to the following line in the song "My Boy, You May Take it From Me" from *Ruddigore* by Gilbert and Sullivan:

ROBIN
I'm diffident, modest and shy.

Ruddigore was the tenth of fourteen comic operas by Gilbert and Sullivan. It opened on 22 January 1887 at the Savoy Theatre. The first night was not altogether a success, as the critics and audience felt that it did not measure up to its predecessor, *The Mikado*. After some changes, including the respelling the title (originally spelt *Ruddygore*), it achieved a run of 288 performances.

40.18 ~ Suffragettes. During 1906, the term Suffragette became associated with the 'Votes for Women' movement whose protests were beginning to move beyond peaceful demonstration. This explains why Mr. Spender remains fearful of them throughout the playlet.

40.34 ~ Mr. Birrill's Bill! Augustine Birrell (1850-1933) was the President of the Board of Education. During 1906, he tabled a Bill that sought to pacify the grievances of Nonconformists over the 1902 Education Act. The House of Commons passed 'Birrill's Bill' but the House of Lords altered it so much that it was withdrawn.

41.7 ~ You will not find our names in Burke. A reference to a book entitled *Burke's Peerage, Baronetage & Knightage 1908: A Genealogical and Heraldic Dictionary of the Peerage and Baronetage, the Privy Council, Knightage and Companionage* (London: Harrison & Sons Ltd.). It was an authoritative, in-depth historical guide to the titled families of the United Kingdom.

41.31 ~ If Dr Clifford were to hear you! Or R. J. Campbell! Both men were leading Nonconformist ministers. They each opposed Birrell's Bill and were held in high public esteem (see **12.11**). The Birrell Bill proposed that after 1 January 1908, no school should be recognised as a public school unless it was funded by the local education authority.

41.36 ~ *Sir H. C.-B.* Henry Campbell-Bannerman was the first Liberal Prime Minister (1905-1908). He was also the first First Lord of the Treasury to use the term Prime Minister as an official title (see **1.30 & 26.12**).

42.11 ~ (LAB. MEM. He *grovels* to Keir Hardie.). James Keir Hardie was the first Labour MP (see **26.17**).

43.3 ~ In this country it is understood that all peers are dissolute and all members of the labouring classes are temperate and pure. This idea is satirised in several Gilbert and Sullivan operas. For example, the following lines are in the song "My Well-Loved Lord and Guardian" from *Iolanthe* (see **38.4**):

PHYLLIS
Nay, tempt me not.
To rank I'll not be bound;
In lowly cot
Alone in virtue found!

43.22 ~ *Song: "The Respectable Peer".* This song is written in the same metre as "My Boy, You May Take it From Me" from *Ruddigore* by Gilbert and Sullivan (see **39.29**).

43.35 ~ **Father Vaughan.** Father Bernard Vaughan (1847-1922) was a Jesuit priest and the brother of Cardinal Herbert Alfred Vaughan (1832-1903). His attacks on immorality of every form earned him the nickname 'the Scourge of Society' (see Figure 31).

Figure 31. Father Bernard Vaughan (c. 1910).

44.40 ~ **No; but they've *read* about peers in Reynolds's.** Reynold's *Weekly News* was a popular Sunday newspaper that combined a 'radical working class approach' with 'sensationalism'.

46.2 ~ If you listen, I will tell you, as concisely as I can. This resonates with the both the title and opening line of the song "If You Give Me Your Attention" from *Princess Ida* by Gilbert and Sullivan (see **3.32**):

KING GAMA
If you give me your attention, I will tell you what I am,
I'm a genuine philanthropist — all other kinds are sham.

46.5 ~ For I am a philanthropist. No other kinds are genuine. Although the metre is slightly different, this line resonates with the second line of the song "If You Give Me Your Attention" from *Princess Ida* (see **46.2**).

47.1 ~ Vous êtes un joli chien. This is a French phrase which, when translated into English means 'you are a pretty dog'. Fletcher Robinson was a Francophile and frequently visited and wrote about France. He also read books that were written in the French language and had reviewed them for the *Daily Express* (1900-1904).

47.11 ~ *Song: Lady Highflyer.* This is a parody of the song "When I was a Lad" from *HMS Pinafore* by Gilbert and Sullivan. This opera was the fourth of their fourteen collaborations and it opened on 25 May 1878 at Opera Comique in London. "Lady Highflyer" reflected Society's horror (but the general public's delight) at the number of musical comedy actresses (Gaiety Girls etc.) marrying into the aristocracy. For example, during 1901 Rosie Boote had become Marchioness of Headfort and Rachel Berridge had married the Earl of Clonmell. In 1905 Anna Robinson became a countess and in 1906, Eva Carrington and Frances Belmont became baronesses. Ironically, Fletcher Robinson married Gladys Hill Morris, a self-proclaimed 'Actress', on 3 June 1902 at St. Barnabas Church in London. She was the daughter of the noted Victorian artist, Philip Richard Morris (1833-1902).

49.31 ~ We hold a lot of Kaffir shares. In the 1890s, many once profitable British companies were producing poor returns. Hence, many investors began speculating in the gold mines of South African instead. However, with the onset of the Second Boer War (1899-1902) and mounting concerns about the treatment of Chinese miners in the Cape colonies (see **36.30**), there was a rapid decline in market confidence and the price of mineral stocks fell sharply. Many shareholders were ruined.

50.7 ~ If railways soon were nationalised. Many British shareholders believed that a socialist government might nationalize the British railway industry. This fear would be realised forty-one years (1 January 1948).

Appendix A

In 1903, Bertram Fletcher Robinson wrote the lyrics for *The John Bull Store Song* (see **5.39**). According to his obituary in the *Daily Express* (26 January 1907), it 'was sung all over England' prior to the landslide Liberal Party victory in the General Election of 1906. These lyrics are interesting for several reasons. Firstly, they do not contain any apparent allusions to the work of W. S. Sullivan. This might suggest that Wodehouse was solely responsible for writing most of the lyrics within the four playlets that are reproduced herein. Secondly, the lyrics betray the fact that Fletcher Robinson was an avid supporter of Joseph Chamberlain. This would explain the Liberal Unionist bias that is particularly apparent within both *The Sleeping Beauty* and *A Winter's Tale*.

Fletcher Robinson's political views were shaped by his family. His late father, Joseph Fletcher Robinson (1827-1903) was a member of Ipplepen Liberal Club and also a close friend of Sir Charles Seale-Hayne (1833-1903), the Liberal MP for Mid-Devonshire (1887-1903). Fletcher Robinson's uncle, Sir John Richard Robinson (1828-1903) was a member of the managing committee of the Liberal Reform Club in London. Following the death of Sir Charles Seale-Hayne (21 November 1903), Fletcher Robinson was short-listed to stand as the Liberal Candidate in the resulting by-election. However, this candidacy was eventually awarded to a local farmer called Harry Trelawney Eve (likely because Fletcher Robinson opposed the Liberal mainstream position on Free Trade). On 8 January 1904, Eve defeated the Unionist Party candidate, General Sir Richard Harrison and won the seat.

The

John Bull Store

song

words by

B. Fletcher Robinson

music by

Robert Eden.

London:
Elkin & Co. Ltd.
8 & 10. Beak Street,
Regent Street. W.

THE JOHN BULL STORE.

Words by
B. FLETCHER ROBINSON.

Music by
ROBERT EDEN.

1. When our Nel-son kept the Bri-tish flag a-fly-ing, When we hammer'd "Bo-ney" on the shore, There were
2. But an al-ter'd tale our pre-sent day is tell-ing. For the Em-pire's glo-ry seems to fade, We are

tra - ders com - ing hat in hand a - buy - ing. At the
buy - ing where we used to go a - sell - ing. And the

coun - ter of the John Bull Store. When we'd beat - en all our foes. Then as
for - eign - er has grabb'd our trade. Just when things are look - ing black. And the

ev - ry bo - dy knows. They were beg - ging for the things we
or - ders get - ting slack. Comes a cham - pion leap - ing to the

made. For the Ger - man, Yank, and Russ, Tho' they
fore, With an eye - glass in his eye, That the

liked to sneer at us. Weren't a patch up-on John Bull at
quick-er he can spy. What is want-ing in the John Bull

trade, _____ Weren't a patch up on John Bull at
store, _____ What is want-ing in the John Bull

trade. } Buy! buy! buy! at the John Bull Store, The
store. }

Deut-scher and the Yank we shall want no more, And the

mon - ey that we gain, Will in Bri - tish hands re - main, If we
buy at the John Bull Store.

CHORUS ad lib.

Buy! buy! buy! at the John Bull Store, The Deut - scher and the Yank we shall want no more. And the mon - ey that we gain, Will in

Bri _ tish hands re _ main. If we buy at the John Bull

Store!

And he's

made a plan to draw our lads to _ ge _ ther. All the

Empire stand-ing hand in hand,— That our trade may grow in fair or e-vil wea-ther. And good for-tune smile up-on our land. Now our "Joe" is straight and square, And he's al-ways played us fair, When we've trust-ed him with jobs be-fore. So let's help him all we can, And we'll

100

find that Jo_ey's plan, Is the sav_ing of the John Bull

Store _____ Is the sav_ing of the John Bull Store.

Buy! buy! buy! at the John Bull Store. The

Deut_scher and the Yank we shall want no more, And the

mon_ey that we gain. Will in Bri_tish hands re_main. If we buy at the John Bull

Store.

Buy! buy! buy! at the John Bull Store. The

Deut_scher and the Yank we shall want no more. And the mon_ey that we gain. Will in

Bri_tish hands re_main. If we buy at the John Bull Store!

Appendix B

On 8 April 1904, the United Kingdom and France signed a series of agreements that are generally referred to as the *Entente cordiale*. This act marked the start of a peaceful co-existence that has continued to date. The importance of these agreements can not be understated as relations between Britain and France were frequently strained throughout the 19th Century. Indeed, the two countries had nearly gone to war in 1898 over a territorial dispute in Eastern Africa ('Fashoda Incident'). The Anglo-French Entente, along with the Anglo-Russian Entente and the Franco-Russian Alliance, later became part of the Triple Entente between the UK, France, and Russia. It paved the way for the diplomatic and military cooperation that preceded the First World War.

In 1904, the Anglo-French Entente was widely welcomed by both English and French citizens and it prompted a series of political exchanges between the two countries. For example, during October 1905, a delegation from the Paris Municipal Council paid a warmly received visit to London (see **38.2**). In February of the following year, a delegation from the London County Council made a reciprocal visit to Paris. The LCC was controlled by the 'Progressive Party', a Liberal/Socialist alliance that was becoming increasingly unpopular amongst Londoners. In contrast, these same citizens felt an unprecedented sense of 'bonhomie' towards the French politicians as is evident in the following article from *The Times* newspaper (Monday 23 October 1905, p. 4):

THE ENTENTE MUNICIPALE.

The Municipal Councillors of Paris left London on Saturday morning for Paris, *via* Dover and Calais, the occasion of their departure from Victoria Station affording their hosts of the London County Council another opportunity to show how cordially they are welcome among us. More than half the members of the Council were at the station, some of them accompanied by their wives, and for half an hour before the departure of the train at 11 o'clock there was an animated scene, the leave-takings indicating unmistakably that real friendships have been formed between the Councillors of the two cities. As the visit was at an end the special Providence in the matter of weather, to which M. Cambon has referred, permitted a few drops of rain, but no more than was sufficient to lay the dust in the roads. Among the members of the London County Council present were :—Mr. E. A. Cornwall (Chairman), Lieutenant-Colonel Clifford Probyn, Mr. Evan Spicer, Captain F. Hemphill, Lord Monkswell, Mr. E. J. Horniman, Mr. Howell J. Williams, Mr. W. E. Mullins, Mr. T. Wiles, Mr. F. W. Verney, the Rev. A. W. Jephson, Mr. S. Sankey, Mr. B. S. Straus, Mr. E. White, Mr. J. Lewis, Mr. T. Davies, Mr. D. S. Waterlow, Mr. Bruce, Mr. G. H. Radford. Among others present may be mentioned Sir Algernon West, Lord Elcho, Mr. G. Laurence Gomme, Sir Roper Parkington, Mr. W. E. Riley, and M. Cambon, who also went to Paris on Saturday, travelling with the party. One or two of the County Councillors wore Tricolor rosettes, a souvenir of Friday's farewell dinner, and the special saloon cars which were attached to the train were labelled in the French colours.

The South-Eastern and Chatham Railway authorities had done what was possible for the comfort of the party. Mr. Green, the superintendent of Victoria Station, having placed the Royal waiting room at their disposal. Here the London County Councillors took their leave of Dr. Brousse, and the Paris Councillors of Mr. Cornwall, with many expressions of gratification at their visit. Mrs. Evan Spicer having presented to Dr. Brousse two enormous chrysanthemums, which were much admired, the President read out the following telegram, which had been received by M. Caire from the French colony in London :—" Vos amis français de Londres vous souhaitent ainsi que votre honoré président et tous vos collègues un bon voyage de retour, et vous disent au revoir." Dr. Brousse and Mr. Cornwall then embraced each other in the French fashion, exchanging kisses on both cheeks, and our visitors took their seats in the train. As it steamed out of the station there was much shaking of hands from the windows, and then cheers on both sides, waving of hats, and cries of " A bientôt " and " Au revoir," in response to the " Bon voyage " of those left on the platform.

The following telegram has been received by Mr. E. A. Cornwall, the Chairman of the London County Council :—

The Municipal Council of Paris, arriving on French territory, salutes Mr. Cornwall, the Chairman of the London County Council, and begs to present to him, to all his colleagues, and to the population which he represents with such dignity, its heartiest thanks for the great reception which was accorded to it.

Vive Londres ! Vive Paris !

PAUL BROUSSE.

We have received the following from the London County Council :—

An act of characteristic courtesy on the part of the Municipal Councillors of Paris marked their departure from Victoria Station. Two beautiful bouquets of enormous size were presented to Mrs. Cornwall and Miss Cornwall by Dr. Brousse, the President of the Paris Council ; while his colleagues made a collection on behalf of Messrs. Hearn's coachmen, to the number of 60, who were employed throughout the week in driving the visitors about the metropolis. The sum collected was considerable ; and, in forwarding the money, Dr. Brousse expressed his appreciation of " the great skill and punctuality of the English coachmen."

Bibliography

Adams, R. J. Q., *Balfour: The Last Grandee*, (London: John Murray, 2007).

Ainger, M., *Gilbert and Sullivan, a Dual Biography*, (Oxford: Oxford University Press, 2002).

Carr, J. D., *The Life of Sir Arthur Conan Doyle*, (London: John Murray, 1949).

Crowther, A., *Contradiction Contradicted: The Plays of W.S. Gilbert*, (Cranbury, New Jersey: Fairleigh Dickinson University Press, 2000).

Day, B. & Ring, T., *Wodehouse In His Own Words*, (New York: The Overlook Press, 2003).

Donaldson, F., *P G Wodehouse: A Biography*, (London: Prion Books, 2001).

Duncan, A., Close to Holmes: *A Look at the Connections between Historical London and Sir Arthur Conan Doyle*, (London: MX Publishing Ltd., 2009).

Edwards, O. D., *P.G. Wodehouse: A Critical and Historical Essay*, (London: Brian and O'Keefe, 1977).

Edwards, O. D., *The Quest for Sherlock Holmes*, (Edinburgh: Mainstream Publishing, 1983).

Jaggard, G., *Blandings the Blest and the Blue Blood: A Companion to the Blandings Castle Saga of P.G. Wodehouse*, (London: Macdonald, 1967).

Jason, D. A., *P.G. Wodehouse: A Portrait of a Master*, (New York: Mason and Lipscomb, 1974).

Jason, D. A., *The Theatre of P.G. Wodehouse*, (London: Batsford Ltd., 1979).

Judd, D., *Radical Joe: A Life of Joseph Chamberlain*, (London: Hamish Hamilton, 1977).

Lellenberg, J., Stashower, D. & Foley, C., *Arthur Conan Doyle: A Life in Letters*, (London: HarperPress, 2007).

Lycett, A., *Conan Doyle: The Man Who Created Sherlock Holmes*, (London: Weidenfeld & Nicolson, 2007).

McCrum, R., *Wodehouse: A Life*, (London: Viking, 2004).

McIlvaine, E., Sherby, L. S. & Heineman, J. H., *P.G. Wodehouse: A Comprehensive Bibliography and Checklist*, (New York: James H. Heineman, Inc., 1990).

Murphy, N. T. P., *A Wodehouse Handbook: The World and Words of P.G. Wodehouse (Two Volume Set)*, (Popgood & Groolley, 2006).

Murphy, N. T. P., *In Search of Blandings: The Facts Behind the Wodehouse Fiction*, (London: Secker & Warburg, 1986).

Pearson, H., *Conan Doyle, his Life and Art*, (London: Macdonald and Jane's, 1977).

Phelps, B., *P G Wodehouse: Man and Myth*, (London: Constable and Co. Ltd., London, 1992).

Pugh, B. W., *A Chronology of the Life of Sir Arthur Conan Doyle – 22nd May 1859 to 7th May 1930*, (London: MX Publishing Ltd., 2009).

Pugh, B. W. & Spiring, P. R., *Bertram Fletcher Robinson: A Footnote to The Hound of the Baskervilles*, (London: MX Publishing Ltd., 2008).

Pugh, B. W. & Spiring, P. R., *On the Trail of Arthur Conan Doyle: An Illustrated Devon Tour*, (Brighton: Book Guild Publishing, 2008).

Ring, T., *The Wit and Wisdom of P.G. Wodehouse*, (London: Arrow Books Ltd., 2008).

Robinson, J. R., *Fifty Years on Fleet Street*, (London: Macmillan & Co., 1904).

Spiring, P. R. (compiler), *Aside Arthur Conan Doyle: Twenty Original Tales by Bertram Fletcher Robinson*, (London: MX Publishing Ltd. 2009).

Spiring, P. R. (compiler), *The World of Vanity Fair by Bertram Fletcher Robinson*, (London: MX Publishing Ltd. 2009).

Stashower, D., *Teller of Tales: The Life of Arthur Conan Doyle*, (New York: Henry Holt & Co., 1999).

Weller, P. L., *The Hound of the Baskervilles: Hunting the Dartmoor Legend*, (Tiverton: Devon Books, 2001).

Wilson, J., *C. B.: Life of Sir Henry Campbell-Bannerman*, (London: Constable & Co., 1973).

Printed in the United Kingdom by
Lightning Source UK Ltd., Milton Keynes
140474UK00001B/6/P